D1559298

LIFE, LOVE,
AND
REPTILES

LIFE, LOVE, AND REPTILES

An Autobiography of
Sherman A. Minton, Jr., M.D.

Foreword by
Kraig Adler, Ph.D.

Krieger Publishing Company
Malabar, Florida
2001

Original edition 2001

Edited by Breck Bartholomew

Printed and Published by
KRIEGER PUBLISHING COMPANY
KRIEGER DRIVE
MALABAR, FL 32950

FROM A DECLARATION OF PRINCIPLES JOINTLY
ADOPTED BY A COMMITTEE OF THE AMERICAN BAR
ASSOCIATION AND A COMMITTEE OF PUBLISHERS:

This publication is designed to provide accurate and authoritative
information in regard to the subject matter covered. It is sold with
the understanding that the publisher is not engaged in rendering
legal, accounting, or other professional service. If legal advice or
other expert assistance is required, the services of a competent professional person should be sought.

Library of Congress Cataloging-in-Publication Data

Minton, Sherman A.
    Life, love, and reptiles : an autobiography of Sherman A. Minton, Jr.,
    M.D. / foreword by Kraig Adler.
       p. cm.
    ISBN 1-57524-172-2 (hardcover : alk. paper)
    1. Minton, Sherman A. 2. Herpetologist—Indiana—Biography.
3. Microbiologist—Indiana—Biography. I. Title.

QL31.M625 A3   2001
597.91'092—dc21

                                   2001038011

10   9   8   7   6   5   4   3   2

To Madge

*remembering the many years we followed
unmarked paths to some curious destinations*

CONTENTS

FOREWORD

BY KRAIG ADLER

Early in the 19th century, America's first professional biologists who worked with amphibians and reptiles were all medical doctors. The M.D. degree program then was the only one that included any advanced training in science or natural history, for the Ph.D. degree was not introduced from Europe until late in the century. Consequently, Benjamin Smith Barton, Jacob Green, Edward Hallowell, Richard Harlan, James E. De Kay, Jared P. Kirtland, D. Humphreys Storer, Gerard Troost, and the father of American herpetology, John Edwards Holbrook, were all medical doctors by training and naturalists by avocation. Ironically, their reputations today rest almost entirely upon their nonmedical work. De Kay, in fact, never practiced medicine at all and Holbrook was so queasy at the sight of blood that he routinely let others take over his surgery once he started.

Today, of course, we take it for granted that professional herpetologists have Ph.D.s. Indeed, most of those trained over the last century have been Ph.D.s, with the exception of a small band of M.D.s who specialized in snakes or venoms or both, and who, like their predecessors of yesteryear, are largely herpetologists by avocation. Sherman Minton was perhaps the best known member of this small group of medical herpetologists, who maintained very close friendships with one another.

This fascinating book is the story of the life and career of an unusual man. His father became prominent in the political and judicial life of Indiana and of the United States—as U.S.

Senator and, later, as an Associate Justice of the U.S. Supreme Court—yet Sherman was one of the most modest and understated biologists of his era. Despite his international reputation, he was always happy to find time to talk at length with the neighborhood children who showed an interest in reptiles or with young students at national meetings. Although Sherman was trained in the laboratory as a microbiologist, he was happiest in the field, especially in his beloved southern Indiana.

Sherman Anthony Minton, Jr. was born the 24th of February 1919 in New Albany, Indiana, just across the Ohio River from Louisville, Kentucky. This is unglaciated, thus hilly, countryside much like that of southern Ohio where I grew up. The area is loaded with herps, mostly eastern species but with a substantial number that entered the region from the mid-South via the Mississippi and Ohio or their predecessor rivers. As Sherman tells us, New Albany at that time had "traces of a Mark Twain-era river town" and some Civil War veterans were still living among its citizenry. It was a genteel place with Southern charm and must have been a bucolic place to grow up.

Like many of us, Sherman's first contact with reptiles were the animals that crawled through his family's backyard or those found in fields at the edge of town. It was his mother, Gertrude, who encouraged his interest in nature. Many of us can relate to his reference to a circus "chameleon," the anoles that were routinely sold at traveling circuses in little boxes and which had leashes around their neck, with pin, allowing them to be attached to one's shirt to enjoy their color changes and other behaviors. In the summer, he went off to camp on Lake Maxinkuckee in northern Indiana, at Culver Military Academy, where he was able to catch the many species of turtles that are so abundant in that area. His autobiography is replete with childhood stories of reptiles and countryside adventures, often in the company of his younger brother, John. He remained faithful to southern Indiana throughout his career and even, as his close friend Bern Bechtel tells us in the final chapter, to his final days. From the vivid descriptions of his childhood there, one can readily see why.

Sherman attended Indiana University, only 80 miles from

Foreword

New Albany, and graduated in 1939 with a degree in zoology. It was here, during his junior year, that he met his future wife, coauthor, and life partner, Madge Rutherford, who was also an amateur naturalist with southern Indiana roots. Sherman went on to Indiana University School of Medicine, staying in Bloomington for the first year and then moving on to Indianapolis. By this time Madge had transferred to Butler University, also in Indianapolis. It was two of his professors in medical school who interested Sherman in microbiology as a specialty, which he later developed into his medical career. But World War II intervened, with Sherman stationed for his internship with the Navy in herpetologically rich San Diego, and Madge in Texas where she joined the newly organized Womens Army Service Pilots (or WASPs) which ferried military planes of all sorts throughout the country. They married in 1943, but their separate military service continued. Sherman was assigned duty aboard the USS *Brooks* and went off to New Guinea and the Philippines, places to which he would return three decades later using SCUBA techniques in search of sea snakes. He was on board the *Brooks* when that ship was involved in the horrific invasion of Luzon Island in the Philippines and was hit by a kamikaze plane.

After the war, and with a continuing interest in a field with which he had had no formal training, Sherman decided to attend the University of Michigan. He was one of that huge number of returning servicemen who received educational training under the so-called GI Bill of Rights, a law passed in 1944. He had already announced his herpetological intentions in his first paper, entitled "Introduction to the Study of the Reptiles of Indiana," published in the *American Midland Naturalist* in 1944. At Michigan, he took the herpetology course taught by Norman E. Hartweg and Charles F. Walker in 1946–1947. Since Sherman had planned to return to Indiana to practice medicine, Hartweg and Walker impressed upon him the need for a modern survey of the amphibians and reptiles of the state. This became a lifelong project that was finally to result in a book nearly three decades later.

Instead of establishing a private medical practice, Sherman accepted a position on the faculty of the Department of

Microbiology and Immunology at Indiana University School of Medicine where he remained until his retirement in 1984. His primary duties were to teach medical microbiology to medical students and others in allied health fields. In addition to microbiology and herpetology, he developed an interest in venomous animals and their venoms, tropical medicine, and parasitology.

All the while, in his spare time, he conducted surveys of the amphibians and reptiles of Indiana in preparation for his book on the topic. And he made some highly interesting discoveries along the way. For example, Sherman found that he could distinguish two different kinds of Jefferson salamanders: a larger, lead-colored form (*Ambystoma jeffersonianum*) and a smaller, blue-spotted form that he recognized as a separate species and for which he resurrected a 100-year-old unused name (*A. laterale*). His results were published in *Herpetologica* in 1954. It was not until the ecological and cytological work of Thomas Uzzell in the 1960s that the genetic differences between these species began to be understood and Sherman's conclusions were confirmed.

Throughout the late 1940s and early 1950s, most of Sherman's herpetological work dealt with Indiana species, but with an increasing interest in the venomous snakes of North America. His Indiana survey work continued and, as one part of it, he published a paper on herpetofaunal distributions in Indiana and Illinois, jointly in 1957 with Philip W. Smith. This paper was important in establishing the role of the postglacial Xerothermic period on the present-day distributions of several species of Indiana's reptiles.

Early in 1958, an unexpected opportunity presented itself. At the request of the International Cooperation Administration (forerunner of the Agency for International Development, or AID), Indiana University established a Basic Medical Science Institute in Karachi, Pakistan (then West Pakistan), which was later to be taken over by the Pakistani government to train medical personnel and is today the Jinnah Postgraduate Medical Center. Sherman was asked to be part of the faculty contingent going over, as the staff microbiologist. As a boy, Sherman had been fascinated by Rudyard Kipling's stories of

Foreword

British India, in his two *Jungle Books,* and the orphaned boy Mowgli, who was instructed by Kaa, the wise python, and of the vicious encounters between Rikki-Tikki-Tavi and the pair of marauding cobras. What herpetologist could not be intrigued with such stories and inspired to see Kipling's India someday? Certainly not Sherman. As he tells us in his autobiography, it was on an icy, snow-swept road in January 1958, on returning from an out-of-town lecture, that he informed Madge: "Darling, that Pakistan project . . . is beginning to look better and better." Indiana herpetology would have to wait. The Indian Subcontinent beckoned. By June they were in Karachi, where they were based until October 1962.

Pakistan then was not well known herpetologically. Except for the early work of James A. Murray in the 1880s, its herpetofauna was covered only incidentally as part of more comprehensive works on the herpetofauna of all of British India by George A. Boulenger (1890) and Malcolm A. Smith (1931–1943). The time was thus ripe for a trained herpetologist to survey the amphibians and reptiles in detail. Sherman published some smaller papers, but his first major paper on the West Pakistani herpetofauna was an extensively annotated and photographically rich key, published in 1962 by the American Museum of Natural History which had appointed him a Research Associate of its Department of Herpetology five years earlier. His major contribution on Pakistan, of course, was a book-length monograph, entitled *A Contribution to the Herpetology of West Pakistan* and published by the museum in 1966. This is a masterful treatise, with an exceptionally good biogeographic analysis covering the nine herpetological divisions of Pakistan recognized by Sherman. It is still the most comprehensive modern herpetology of that country. In all, the Mintons had traveled some 43,000 miles and collected more than 1,500 specimens during their more than four years in Pakistan. This was a family effort, in which Madge was Sherman's primary support person, but their three daughters— Brooks, April, and Holly—provided a team of ready and willing field assistants. Madge paid special attention to anthropology and archaeology, and during their collecting trips to southern Baluchistan, the Mintons discovered an ancient ceremonial site that had been active in 2000 B.C.

On returning to Indianapolis in 1962, he resumed his professorship at the medical school. Much of his research during the next years was on venomous snakes and he produced two books: *Venomous Reptiles* in 1969, coauthored with Madge, and *Snake Venoms and Envenomation,* which he edited in 1971. The former was issued in a revised edition in 1980. Nevertheless, his other herpetological interests were not neglected and, in 1972, he finally published the results of three decades of local work in his book, *Amphibians and Reptiles of Indiana* (another more definitive edition is due for publication this year). The next year, with Madge, he published what is perhaps their best known work to the general public, *Giant Reptiles.* This drew heavily upon their own observations, especially those made in Pakistan. Another book, *Venom Disease,* followed in 1974; this is an excellent textbook of medical toxicology.

It is difficult to summarize Sherman's research accomplishments succinctly, for they are extremely diverse in terms of subject matter and in terms of geography. Doubtless this is due to the fact that he was, by profession, a microbiologist, and thus, beyond this specialization, he was free to choose whatever interested him. Thus, we see papers on the herpetofauna of the Big Bend region of Texas, on Mexico and Central America; on the sea snakes of Southeast Asia and the South Pacific; on toxic bites by rear-fanged snakes; on biochemical properties of snake venoms; on relationships of groups of snakes based on immunology; plus numerous articles throughout his career that were intended for amateur and professional snake keepers. He was one of the most vociferous opponents of the quack therapy for electric shock treatment for snakebites. Through his studies in the early 1950s, he was able to show that the original antivenin developed by Wyeth Laboratories was not effective against the venoms of the major North American pit vipers, leading Wyeth to significantly improve their crotalid antivenin in a way that then went unchanged for nearly half a century.

Sherman was the first to note that the venom of the Mojave rattlesnake (*Crotalus scutulatus*) was ten times more toxic, in terms of its LD_{50} values for mice, in the Big Bend region than it was in snakes from the central part of the species' range.

Foreword

This demonstration of geographic variation in venom toxicity is of unknown significance but is the subject of active investigation today. And so on. The same themes, even those begun early in his career, continued to reappear: Indiana herpetology, venomous snakes, snake venoms, snakebite. He even continued to publish sporadically on Asian herpetology, including a book, *Handbook to Middle East Amphibians and Reptiles,* coauthored with Alan E. Leviton, Steven C. Anderson, and myself in 1992, in the aftermath of the military operations called Desert Storm.

Beyond his own research, Sherman always displayed an exceptional dedication to public service. As but one example, I note the publication in 1962 of the manual, *Poisonous Snakes of the World.* This was issued by the Office of Naval Intelligence for use in training United States amphibious forces, not an unimportant document given America's rapidly increasing commitments in Southeast Asia in the 1960s. Unfortunately, this was an uncritical compilation from the literature. The job must have been assigned to some underling to finish by some arbitrary deadline. The well-known monograph on sea snakes by Malcolm Smith and that by Klauber on rattlesnakes were not cited at all. The manual reported cottonmouths from Massachusetts (but not Florida) and pelagic sea snakes from landlocked Afghanistan! The snakebite section was little better. The Navy, realizing its error, soon withdrew the book from circulation and stocks were destroyed, but Sherman recognized the great value of having a proper manual on poisonous snakes. Perhaps because of his former naval duties, he volunteered, together with Herndon G. Dowling and Findlay E. Russell, to revise the book; Sherman served as chair of the writing committee. A manuscript was duly delivered in November 1965 and their book, which received laudatory reviews, was published in 1968.

Sherman participated in several expeditions—three of them sponsored by the Scripps Institution of Oceanography—to marine waters from the Great Barrier Reef of northeastern Australia to the Philippines to study sea snakes. He joined an American Museum expedition to Iran. He was a consultant on snakebite and other envenomations to several major zoos and poison information centers, further examples of his public service ethic. He was also an official delegate to scientific congresses in Europe, Asia, and South America.

Many honors were bestowed on Sherman in recognition of his scientific accomplishments. He served on the editorial boards of several journals, including *Toxicon* and *Clinical Toxicology*. He was a member of the Board of Governors of the American Society of Ichthyologists and Herpetologists. He served as president of both the International Society of Toxinology and of the Society for the Study of Amphibians and Reptiles. The former awarded him its highest prize—the Redi Award—in 1985, given in recognition of an outstanding career in the field of toxicology.

The Redi Award, in fact, was a particularly fitting prize because the life of its namesake mirrored many facets of Sherman's own career. Francesco Redi was a 17th century physician and biologist who is best remembered for his studies discrediting spontaneous generation, but who also performed the first scientific experiments on snakebite. Like Redi, Sherman had a career that integrated medicine, experimental biology, toxinology, and herpetology. Indeed, there was no one among his own generation who better displayed this combination of talents, to which Sherman added still more: an unusual ability to write books for the general public and a dedication to public service. Despite his high reputation as a scientist and the great respect accorded to him by his colleagues, Sherman Minton remained a modest man throughout. What more could one fairly want or expect from a single life?

ACKNOWLEDGMENTS

Special thanks to Kraig Adler, Steven Anderson, H. Bernard Bechtel, Harold G. Cogger, Roger Conant, Carl Gans, Harold Heatwole, and Muhammad Sharif Khan for their contributions to this book.

Madge Rutherford Minton has been particularly helpful and patient during the preparation of this book. Not only has she generously provided information and photographs, but she opened her doors to us to sort through many of Sherman's photographs and letters.

We also thank Breck Bartholomew for his efforts in soliciting and compiling the vignettes, photo placements, and providing electronic files of the text.

Madge is thankful to Bern Bechtel and Dave Hardy for all their help.

CHAPTER 1
NEW ALBANY, INDIANA

Long ago in the 1950s, I regularly got invitations to talk to Boy Scouts, 4-H Clubs, junior high school science clubs, and similar groups. Almost always, someone in the audience would ask, "Are you a real doctor?" I often wanted to say, "No, I'm just a figment of your imagination. Take two aspirin and I'll disappear."

However, I understood why they asked. Real doctors in 1950 did not give talks about snakes. Real doctors treated sick people except on Wednesday afternoons when they played golf. They drove Buicks and belonged to the country club. They did not have turtles wandering about their house, nor did they drive fifty miles to listen to a chorus of frogs.

About that time, I was working on the reptiles and amphibians of Indiana, and I would often stop in a county seat town for a meal or cold drink looking as though I had just dropped off the freight train. Occasionally I would meet a medical school classmate, now the bright young physician of the community. Probably he, too, wondered if I was a real doctor.

It was my fate to be born in a borderland. New Albany, Indiana, is an Ohio River town directly across from Louisville, Kentucky. Although it had an identity of its own in 1919, New Albany was economically and culturally closer to Louisville than to upstate Indiana. It still had traces of a Mark Twain-era river town. There were whitewashed fences, and boys swam in the river despite dangers of drowning or catching typhoid fever. I recall the sound of the steamboat calliope on the summer air, and my first trip to Cincinnati was made by riverboat. Among

Sherman teaching a group of school kids

the town's oldest citizens were Civil War veterans of both sides. Much of southern Indiana is hilly, and just west of New Albany is a conspicuous ridge, the knobstone escarpment, that we who lived there knew just as "the knobs."

I was born on February 24, 1919, in a comfortable house on Market Street near the center of New Albany. At that time, my father was serving with the army in France, and my mother was living with her relatives who were dressmakers. This was the winter of the devastating influenza epidemic, and she'd hardly gotten over the flu when I chose to appear. One February, a few weeks after the great midwestern blizzard, my mother wrote me, "Believe it or not, on your real birthday I could look across the street and see flowers blooming in Krementz's yard. I shall be thinking of you on the 24th."

Both my parents were born in little farm communities near New Albany, but my father's family moved to Fort Worth, Texas, when he was a boy. I saw my Texas relatives only sporadically during my early years. However, my mother's parents lived on a small farm near DePauw, about thirty miles northwest of New Albany by train. We visited them regularly, and a good deal of my early knowledge of natural history was acquired on their farm.

New Albany, Indiana

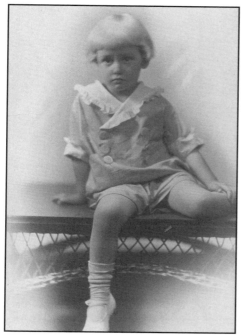
Sherman about 1921

My father came home from France in the spring of 1919 and resumed his practice of law as a partner in a local firm. We continued to live in what my parents for the rest of their lives called "The Old House" until my sister, Mary Anne, arrived. She appeared some weeks prematurely and there was concern about her survival. Inherent toughness and good nursing care were the only things a premature infant had going for it in those days. Soon afterward, we moved into a house of our own. A few years later, my brother, John, was born. Medical practice and possibly family finances had changed enough that he was born in the local hospital.

I can't remember a time when I wasn't fascinated by animals, particularly the ones that most people feared or disliked. Creatures like the big dragonflies (devil's darning needles or snake-feeders) and praying mantis (devil's race-horses) were regarded with suspicion. My mother had a marked fear of the large moth larvae that occasionally appeared in late summer, and this probably led to my having an irrational fear of caterpillars that lasted many years. Traces of it still remain. Ladybugs, fireflies, and the big metallic green beetles we called Junebugs were more acceptable insects that I was allowed to catch and keep in glass jars. I also collected molted cicada skins (locust shells, if you lived in southern Indiana) and once got an adult cicada released by a huge digger wasp. Most surprisingly, a box turtle ambled into our yard one morning. I suspect it was one that someone had caught in the countryside and released in town, although in those days there may have been a few free-living box turtles in New Albany. In the center of town was a large farmers' market with rows of stalls in a long, low, brick building. Country people occasionally brought in big snapping turtles to sell for food; sometimes they brought small turtles of other species as well. These could be bought for a few cents, but few wanted them.

Well before I entered school, much of my interest had centered on reptiles. A family friend gave me a baby alligator, in the 1920s a standard souvenir of a visit to Florida. About the same time, I acquired a "chameleon," the green anole of the southern U.S., probably purchased at one of the small circuses that occasionally visited New Albany. Neither animal survived long. No one I knew had any idea how to keep such creatures in captivity. The first snake I saw was a garter snake my father killed on the golf links at the country club. Near the clubhouse was a grove of trees where children were deposited to play while their parents were on the links. Here, very much alive, I found a slender, bright green snake. My father identified it as a grass snake; the only local species he was quite sure was harmless.

As junior member of his law firm, my father evidently got a lot of scut work, much of which involved driving into the rural areas to interview clients and witnesses. Sometimes he took me with him. Our car was a hand-cranked Ford; roads were poor, and flat tires routine. Changing a tire was quite an operation, for the tube had to be removed and patched, replaced in the casing, and reinflated. Friendly bystanders usually helped, and I thought it was fun, especially since I could poke about in the weeds and creeks while they worked. Some time during that period, my father took my mother and me to see a large snake he'd killed on the Corydon Pike about two miles outside town. The snake, still lying in the road, looked huge. I suppose it may have been no more than four feet long. I recall it as being predominantly whitish, but it may have been lying belly up. I doubt that it was a cow snake (black rat snake in

4

today's field guides) or black racer, the two common big snakes of the area, for I don't think my father would have considered either of these worth cranking up the car for a special trip. Had it been a rattlesnake—there were still a few near New Albany in those days—he'd probably have kept the rattles and told the story of its killing for years. Instead he could not really remember the incident when I asked him about it several years later. I still wonder about the identity of that snake.

The grade school I attended usually had students of two grades in one room, so I could often finish my assigned work and recite with the higher grade. For this reason, I was able to complete eight grades in six school years. This pleased my parents and probably saved me some months of boredom, but it launched me into high school considerably younger than my classmates and behind them in social and athletic skills. In 1928 we moved from Market Street to Silver Hills, a suburb on the crest of the knobstone escarpment just outside New Albany. To the north and west of Silver Hills were miles of hilly country covered with woods and small farms, and threaded by little rocky creeks. Transport to school was by a little trolley car that made the round trip to town every hour. The car stops were in patches of woods where I often saw snakes and lizards while waiting for the car. Silver Hills was about as close to heaven as I'd gotten to date. On Saturdays and holidays, my mother would fill my canteen with lemonade if the weather was hot or cocoa if it was cold, give me a couple of peanut butter and jelly sandwiches, and send me off to trudge the footpaths and gravel roads until I was tired. As I recall, she gave me only two warnings, "Be careful of copperheads!" and "If you see a still, don't go near it!" My mother knew what a copperhead looked like, but she wouldn't have known a still from a Methodist church. It was about five years before I encountered a live copperhead, and I never stumbled onto a still.

Although stills were well concealed, there was considerable evidence of their product. At pull-offs along little-traveled country roads, you often saw unlabeled bottles containing traces of moonshine or white mule. Occasionally, used condoms were seen scattered about, and an older companion explained to me the use of these devices. The depravity that went on at these roadside trysting places was a common topic of conversation among us schoolboys. Living in a rural area, it was hard to overlook the sexual activities of animals, and older boys supplied additional information relating this to human beings. Because the account of reproduction in the *Encyclopaedia Britannica* was right next to the account of reptiles, I almost accidentally acquired some accurate if somewhat austere information on the topic. Sex education in high school consisted of a lecture by the football coach to the boys warning about the dangers of self-abuse and venereal disease. I think the girls got a comparable lecture from someone, but I never heard any details. Nearly every year there were rumors some high school girl had "gotten in trouble." Marriage, often unhappy, was the approved solution for this.

As preteens, most of us experimented with smoking corn silk, catalpa beans, grapevine, and other vegetable material that would smolder. Eventually we tried tobacco. In the little country stores, a corncob pipe cost a nickel and a small bag of Bull Durham an additional dime or so. Cigarettes cost fifteen to twenty cents a pack. Drinking was uncommon among the high school set, partly because liquor was both illegal and expensive. Some families made their own home brewed beer and wine, and this was occasionally sampled. The thought of using mind-altering drugs was so bizarre we never considered it, although there was a persistent rumor you could get drunk on a mixture of aspirin and Coca-Cola.

Adolescence is a dicey time at best, and my academic advancement did not contribute to my adjustment during this period. In 1931, we moved from Silver Hills back to Market Street, probably for economic reasons. This was not difficult because I still had friends there and retained my friends on the hill. It did make my access to the backcountry a little more difficult. Most of my friends were boys who lived near me, and we made up a gang of seven to twelve depending a bit on the activity in which we were engaged. The conventional sports of softball, basketball, and touch football were all played on vacant lots or in the Williamson family's backyard with no adult supervision and minimal equipment. Spring brought marbles and kites. Firecracker wars began about July first if the stores were

New Albany, Indiana

Sherman (in the white pants) and his gang
in New Albany, Indiana

selling munitions. Green apples drilled to hold small firecrackers made fine grenades, belts of little Chinese ladycrackers
sounded like machine gun fire, and bigger firecrackers could lob
empty tin cans high in the air. The more elaborate and expensive
items like Roman candles, pinwheels, and skyrockets were purchased by our fathers and reserved for the night of July Fourth.
Each year there were casualties, usually burns on the hands or
face or sore fingers from things that exploded prematurely. Dr.
Easley, our neighborhood physician, was kept busy.

We had some games that were largely of our own making.
"Hodag" was a sort of paper chase in which one team laid a
trail of code notes and chalk marks for the other to follow.
"Little Men" was a kind of paper doll play, although we'd have
tried to kill anyone who'd have suggested this. The men were
male figures hand-drawn on cardboard or cut from comic strips
and pasted on cardboard. They lived in cities made of bricks
and old boxes or in underground hideouts. Their sole activities
were war and violent crime. There were elaborate rules that

I've mostly forgotten but were taken quite seriously. Once Mrs. Powell, in the course of housecleaning, found Frank's most prized "little man," the "Leader of Tarzans," in his secret hiding place and left him on the kitchen table where he was gleefully captured by a rival gang and held for ransom. The legality of this capture was hotly debated for some days. Once when my brother was slightly delirious from a high fever, my mother asked me, "What's on Johnny's mind? He keeps talking about the men in the secret."

Our Market Street gang had no distinctive clothing or even a name, but each of us had his personal mark or cipher. We used these for years, even into World War II. We had a rival gang we called the River Rats who lived in houses along the edge of the river and in houseboats. One summer we waged a desultory war with them. It was mostly name-calling and an occasional fist fight, but once or twice we used our air rifles against their slingshots. I learned then that wars are not necessarily won by the side with the most sophisticated weapons, but more likely by the side defending its turf. In August, our leader, John Williamson, and their leader, Herbie Stevens, met at a peace conference. Herbie's elder brother acted as a sort of arbitrator. He had been in the Navy and had a tattoo of a naked woman on his leg. We inspected this, exchanged some notes on the sexual mores of our groups, and parted amicably.

It was not too difficult to convince some of my friends that hunting reptiles was interesting and exciting. Most boys in the community fished or hunted; our game was just less conventional. We often walked up to fifteen miles a day hunting in the hills near New Albany. Occasionally, if parents with a car cooperated, we would camp overnight. By 1935 we had collected most of the reptiles known from the region; in fact we collected two species that had not previously been reported in Indiana. Most of our captives were kept a few days and released, for feeding them was a problem. Not infrequently they escaped. One memorable day, John and Donald Williamson caught about twenty banded water snakes in Little Indian Creek and left them in a cardboard box in our backyard. All escaped, and the neighborhood was plagued with snakes until the frosts came. One snake was found crawling up the aisle of the near-

New Albany, Indiana

Sherman (holding the rifle), with friends in
New Albany, Indiana

by Catholic church. Turtle racing was another activity result-
ing from our reptile hunts. Box turtles were plentiful, and
during dry periods they congregated around pools of water that
remained in the little creeks. We brought them into town,
raced them in large circular rings, and kept the fastest. These
were allowed to wander about the neighborhood, and some survived several years. The last ones disappeared after the Great
Flood of 1937 inundated much of New Albany.

There were no science courses in the grade school I attended, but in the ninth grade I had one under Miss Helen White.
She was the sort of enthusiastic, well-informed teacher everyone should have at least once in high school. She explained to
me the significance and importance of scientific nomenclature;
previously those unpronounceable Latin names and enigmatic
abbreviations in some of my books had meant nothing. She
introduced me to animals like the hellbender and brook lam-
prey that were brought to her classes, and gave me a tiny
exotic lizard that was found in Correo's fruit market. I believe

it was one of the Neotropical geckos, probably *Sphaerodactylus* or *Gonatodes*. By contrast, my biology teacher in senior high school was pedantic and stupid. He seemed to have little interest in his subject nor much knowledge of it either. He told us quite emphatically that moles were rodents.

In 1931 New Albany Junior High School housed a surprisingly large natural history collection that had previously been in Borden Institute, a short-lived little college in the town of Borden about fifteen miles northwest of New Albany. Specimens were dispersed through the classrooms without much regard for the subjects being taught. So while our English class discussed *Ivanhoe* and the *Merchant of Venice,* I could look at two museum jars each holding a timber rattlesnake, one with its mouth open to expose an impressive pair of fangs. These were the first rattlesnakes I remember seeing at really close range. About that time, one of my burning ambitions was to catch a timber rattler.

I reasoned, probably correctly, that the snakes had come from the Borden Knobs, an arc of hills extending from Borden northeast toward Henryville.

The tops of the knobs were farmed, but the slopes were almost unbroken forests with occasional rock outcrops. They were also a long way from home. A couple of times, I walked the whole distance. A better tactic was to take the morning train from New Albany to Borden and return in the evening. This gave me most of the day in the hills

Sherman, in 1932, with the first milk snake he ever caught

10

New Albany, Indiana

where I thought the rattlers ought to be. Many of the farmers had rattlesnake stories to tell, but few had seen the snakes. I talked with only one man who had actually killed a rattler during the same year I'd spoken with him. I had no success at all, and it was about seven years later that I caught my first rattlesnake in Indiana. This was in Morgan-Monroe State Forest much to the north. I'd camped at an abandoned farmhouse and was working my way up a hillside when I saw a good-sized male timber rattler in a classic circular coil on the forest floor. This is still one of my most vivid herpetological memories. He didn't rattle until I'd pinned his head and lifted him off the ground.

I learned to read early and have always been an acquirer of books. Soon after I entered school, my father's senior law partner gave me *The Animal Kingdom Illustrated,* a two-volume version of Alvin Johnson's 1879 *Natural History*. It had many highly dramatic engravings—a woman in a horse-drawn sleigh about to throw her children to wolves, a lion crouched over a prostrate hunter, a giant snake constricting a jaguar. These excited my imagination as well as those of my daughters a generation later. For graduation from the eighth grade, my parents gave me a copy of Raymond L. Ditmars' *Reptile Book,* an account of the species native to the United States. It is a readable and well-illustrated book that helped launch the careers of many herpetologists of my generation. Later "Aunt Ella," a family friend with connections in a Louisville bookstore, gave me each new Ditmars book that appeared. Parents and friends gave me other natural history books until I had the nucleus of a personal library when I graduated from college. For Christmas 1942, a beautiful girl who married me about a year later gave me Karl Schmidt and Dwight Davis' *Field Book of Snakes*. About thirteen years later, the authors of this book unrolled their sleeping bags on the front porch of our temporary home in west Texas. The same beautiful girl gave me an unbelievable gift on one of our first Christmases after World War II, three volumes of the first edition of John E. Holbrook's *North American Herpetology*. She bought them from a secondhand book dealer for $50. This book is to herpetology as Audubon is to ornithology except it is far more scarce, complete four-volume sets being almost unknown. The second edition is better known but nevertheless very rare

11

and expensive. The period just after the war was a good time to buy old books; many of the classics in herpetology could be obtained very cheaply. Library discards—usually damaged duplicate copies—were another inexpensive source of books. Charles M. Bogert gave me several valuable books from the American Museum of Natural History, and my daughter, Brooks, gave me books salvaged from the Earlham College library. Today, herpetological books and books by herpetologists appear in ever increasing numbers. The level of science in them is usually more sophisticated, and techniques of illustration are much better, but their cost often spirals out of sight. Tomorrow, it is said, all the world's literature will be instantaneously available on computers, but looking at the books on my shelves is almost like seeing faces of old friends.

By the time I graduated from high school, my parents were somewhat worried about my interest in reptiles. I think they may have seen me as a carnival performer or the owner of a roadside zoo—at the very best a teacher in an obscure college. My father, who had been elected to the U.S. Senate in 1934, tried to interest me in the legal profession with no discernable success. So when I entered college, he made it clear that I would take a premedical course if I expected any support from him. As a compromise, I was allowed to take an undergraduate major in zoology. I entered Indiana University in the fall of 1935 and was pledged to Phi Delta Theta fraternity. This was partly because my father had been a Phi Delt, and partly because I had a good academic record in high school and the frat needed a few like me to keep their grade point average above the acceptable minimum. I was anything but the typical fraternity boy of the 1930s. My dress, grooming, and attitude earned me quite a few paddlings as a freshman; later they just asked me to take a long hike when important guests were expected at the house. I enjoyed interfraternity athletics, especially track and swimming, and the general horseplay, but the social life was painful. The sleek, sophisticated sorority girls terrified me until one afternoon in my junior year.

November 13, 1937, was the most important day of my university career and perhaps of my life. Delta Gamma sorority had invited the Phi Delts to a tea dance, and I went along because I didn't have anything very important to do. Almost at the sorority house door I was met by a tall girl wearing a green velvet dress. Her blond hair was in two little curls on her forehead, and she had a breathtaking figure—in a popular phrase of the day, she was stacked. "Hello," she said, "I understand you collect snakes." I'd had girls use this conversational gambit before. They usually said it about the way you'd say, "I understand you're a hermaphrodite." But this girl was different. Within a few minutes we were arguing about the differences

Sherman and Madge in New Albany, Indiana

between eastern and western painted turtles. Her name was Madge Rutherford, and her father taught zoology at Arsenal Technical High School in Indianapolis. Natural history was but one of her many interests. Before the afternoon was over, we'd made a date for the next weekend. When I arrived at the Delta Gamma house, I found I'd left my billfold behind. I borrowed a dollar from a fraternity brother who was also waiting for his date. Madge and I took a taxi to downtown Bloomington, went to a movie, and had a chocolate soda after which we walked back to the campus. A dollar went just so far even in 1937. This was the beginning of a turbulent six-year courtship. Although she now lived in Indianapolis, Madge also had a southern Indiana background, having grown up in the little quarry town of Saint Paul. We enjoyed the same things, and whatever we did together—dancing, swimming, going to a play, hunting snakes— it was always great fun. We could talk to each other about anything, although we sometimes held quite different opinions. We had some of the same adolescent misgivings—several decades hence they would be called hang-ups and sometimes this led to tears and angry words. But each time we threatened to split, we came back together a little more firmly bonded than before.

Zoology at Indiana University in 1935 was more laboratory than field oriented, and I found the basic courses rather dull. However, I later signed up for courses in evolution, taxonomy, and entomology under Professor Alfred C. Kinsey. Madge took his course in ornithology. His classes were small and informal. He was an interesting and inspiring teacher, although a little short on humor. The entomology course involved a good deal of fieldwork. At that time, garter gnakes, zigzag salamanders, and an occasional black racer could be found on campus, while many other species of amphibians and reptiles lived in the nearby countryside, so entomology field trips often had her-petological fringe benefits. Kinsey had high regard for the taxonomic studies of Alexander Ruthven on garter snakes and Frank Blanchard on kingsnakes, and recommended them to his students. It was the first time I heard these names that would later became familiar to me. Kinsey was just beginning the surveys of human sexual behavior that would make him famous. He relied heavily on his students for his early interviews, and I agreed to be one of his interviewees. I don't know if he kept up the practice or not, but in the early interviews he was willing to answer questions as well as ask them. What I remember best about the interview is being assured that things I'd done and worried about were quite normal. Some of my fraternity brothers bragged about atrocious lies they'd told Kinsey, but I doubt if many of them fooled him. He was a very astute interviewer. When *Sexual Behavior in the Human Male* appeared, I promptly bought a copy and found I fell near the middle of most of the bell-shaped curves in the book.

In 1938 I was accepted for medical school. At that time, the first year was at Bloomington, and my college life changed little. I found the first year courses, particularly gross anatomy, exceptionally tedious. Meanwhile, Madge had transferred to Butler University in Indianapolis where she was establishing a reputation with her poetry. The next year, I moved to Indianapolis to complete my medical education. It was my first experience living in a relatively big city. I didn't like the smog, the traffic, the dirty streams, and the inaccessibility of the countryside. I roomed in homes in downtown Indianapolis and often walked to the medical school. This was quite safe, even after dark.

During the summer of 1939, I had a job as a field assistant on a General Land Office surveying crew in the Colorado mountains. When we were in the high country around Monarch and Marshall Passes, the scenery was impressive and I saw pikas, mountain sheep, and other wildlife new to me, but the only reptile was a garter snake. Later we moved to lower dry, brushy country near Salida, and one evening as three of us were walking back to camp, we were brought up short by the unmistakable whir of a rattler. We quickly spotted a large prairie rattlesnake coiled under a bush and ready for trouble. Using skills learned catching copperheads in Indiana, I captured the snake. The rest of the survey crew were by no means happy with the idea of having a rattlesnake as camp mascot, so that evening I walked to Salida, bought a large bottle of alcohol of the undrinkable sort, and made a preserved specimen of my catch. I still have it. During the next four or five days as we were working, we encountered several more rattlers. All ended up as belt decorations or hatbands. Early in September, war broke out in Europe. About two weeks later when us college dudes left the party, a buddy saw me to the railroad station. "So long, Minton," he said, "See you in the trenches!"

Madge worked that summer in one of the Indiana state parks, and when she returned to college, her principal interest shifted to aviation. There were courses offered at Butler, but considerable consternation ensued when she signed up for them. First she was permitted to take ground school and preliminary but not advanced flight training. She forthrightly wrote Eleanor Roosevelt that she was being discriminated against because of her sex. Mrs. Roosevelt intervened, and Madge got her flight training. She handled the planes as well as any of her male classmates. The university forgot its objections, and she became known as "Butler's flying coed."

In 1940 I had a summer job as naturalist at McCormick's Creek State Park in southern Indiana. My principal job was to take park guests and campers on nature hikes. My knowledge of birds was pretty weak and of wildflowers and plants worse, but I learned quickly from Edna Banta, the chief naturalist. She was a botanist and a good teacher. On most hikes, I could find a snake or salamander that always got peoples' attention. I also helped with care of the wildlife exhibit, and once this entailed removing the scent glands from a litter of baby skunks. My reference book said this could be done without anesthesia. With the animal immobilized by wrapping it in cloth, I made cuts at the edge of the anus and extracted the glands, which were about the size of hazelnuts. I wore only swim trunks and a head cover but was quite pungent at the end of the surgery. My operative mortality was zero.

Medical school courses at Indianapolis were more interesting than those at Bloomington. My favorite was Dr. Thurman B. Rice's bacteriology course. He had a great fund of stories about the history, diagnosis, and prevention of infectious diseases and the part they have played in human affairs. Dr. Rice's temper tantrums were legendary. During one of his lectures, someone catapulted a pellet of metal foil in his direction.

16

New Albany, Indiana

Proudly displaying the descented skunks after his first
attempt at surgery

It hit a lampshade with a gratifying ping, and the volcano erupted. He smashed his pointer on the lectern and called us morons and cowards unworthy to practice the healing arts. He went on to say an unusually rigorous final exam might correct the latter situation. Like many persons of choleric temperament, his rage evaporated quickly. The next lecture was in his usual chatty style, and the exam was no more difficult than others.

When I see the elaborate precautions we now take to prevent bacteriology students from laboratory infections, I cringe at some of the things that were done in Rice's laboratory. A petri dish containing sputum or a piece of pus-soaked bandage would be placed on a bench next to a Bunsen burner and students were expected to make smears and identify the bacteria they saw. Unknown cultures we students were expected to identify could contain bacteria causing meningitis, scarlet fever, pneumonia, typhoid, or bacillary dysentery. If we needed blood agar, a culture medium widely used in diagnostic bacteriology, we bled each other—all this in an era before antibiotics.

I did so well in bacteriology that Dr. Rice asked me to be a student assistant in the course during my junior and senior years. This was my introduction to research and academic medicine. Of the faculty members in the bacteriology department, Dr. Lyle Weed was most interested in research. Medical students disliked him because he was a strict grader and biting and sarcastic in his criticism, but as a fellow worker he was totally different, very patient and considerate. I helped him with some of his research, and he listed me as junior author on two papers, the first time my name appeared in the scientific literature. Dr. Donald White was more clinically oriented and later became a specialist in allergy. He, too, could be pretty caustic. Weed and I were Democrats; White, like most of the faculty, was a Republican. When we walked into the lab after Franklin Roosevelt had been elected to his third term, White's greeting was, "Good morning pallbearers of personal liberty." Harold Raidt, a young bacteriologist trained at the University of Kentucky, was another member of the faculty. He stayed on to become one of the school's best-liked and most innovative teachers.

18

New Albany, Indiana

Late in 1941 I won a prize for an essay, "The Role of the Spleen in Immunity." As I recall, it was $20. The following Saturday night, Madge and I spent the prize money on a trip to Cincinnati. We went to the Netherland Plaza Hotel, which had good food and a dance band. Shortly after midnight, we left and drove back to Indianapolis to our chaste and separate beds. The next morning we awoke to news of bombs falling on Pearl Harbor. The United States was at war.

CHAPTER 2
WORLD WAR II

The war didn't affect me immediately. Being a medical student, I was exempt from the draft, and in the spring of 1941 I'd joined the Naval Reserve. After Pearl Harbor, the medical school program was accelerated with more class hours and no summer vacation. In my senior year, I applied for a Navy internship. This was not pure patriotism. In 1942 a civilian internship might pay $10 a month plus maintenance, but a Navy intern received the pay and allowances of a lieutenant (j.g.), enough that Madge and I could get married.

About this time, I first met a professional herpetologist, Dr. William M. Clay of the University of Louisville, who received his Ph.D. from the University of Michigan for his studies on North American water snakes. He was a quiet, gracious, scholarly person willing to talk for hours about reptiles. He encouraged me to publish my first herpetological paper—an ambitious review of the reptiles of Indiana based largely on my fieldwork. I had only a vague idea of how to write a scientific paper, and the manuscript I submitted to *The American Midland Naturalist* was terribly amateurish. It would never have seen print except for the editorial help of Karl P. Schmidt of the Field Museum, who had great sympathy for amateur naturalists and for young scientists whose careers were being interrupted by the war. Dr. Clay and I remained friends and saw each other regularly but infrequently until his death in 1983.

After I'd been accepted by Madge as a future husband and by the Navy as an intern, I was asked to list my preferences for a duty station. The hospitals I chose were all along the

Sherman with his dog after joining the Navy

southern edge of the nation where I thought the snakes ought
to be. I graduated in December 1942, was assigned to San
Diego, and reported for duty in January 1943.

San Diego Naval Hospital at that time had overflowed its
boundaries and taken in much of Balboa Park, bringing it
cheek-by-jowl with the San Diego Zoo. This made it easy for
me to visit the zoo and, of course, the reptile house. The curator of reptiles was C.B. (Si) Perkins, a most kindly man, —
although he had a command of invective worthy of a bosun's
mate. This was usually directed at people who rapped on the
glass of his snake cages. Despite shortages of personnel, supplies, and equipment, he maintained throughout the war
years the high standards of animal care for which the San
Diego Zoo has always been famous. Perkins told me of good
collecting sites near San Diego, and after the war sent me
specimens of snakes I'd been unable to collect when I was
stationed there. Best of all, he gave me many of the publica-

tions of the San Diego Society of Natural History. One day I met a rugged but distinguished looking man at the reptile house. He was introduced to me as Laurence M. Klauber whose studies of southwestern reptiles, particularly rattlesnakes, were changing the course of herpetology. Like Kinsey, he was a pioneer in using statistical methods to help solve taxonomic problems.

A medical internship is traditionally a time of stress and

Medical school graduation

hardship, but the one at San Diego Naval Hospital had some nice features. About once a week you had all-night duty in the emergency room, "awake and in uniform," an unnecessary qualification, for you never had time to sleep. However, you had the next twenty-four hours completely free. I usually used this time and my gasoline ration to drive to some likely collecting site in San Diego County. The first trips were not very exciting. I found many small salamanders looking like pieces of dark spaghetti, some ordinary looking lizards, a ringneck snake, and a baby gopher snake. About the end of March, things changed suddenly. Within an hour or two in Mission Gorge, I found a mating pair of alligator lizards, several slim, sleek, striped racers, a silvery gray snake that was my first California boa, and a southern Pacific rattlesnake. This was the commonest rattler of the area and could sometimes be found well within the city limits. The biggest rattler was the red diamondback, which was fairly common in the foothills. Perkins told me it was a sluggish, placid snake, but the first one I found was anything but that. It was coiled on a steep, rocky hillside, and when I approached it rose in the spectacular fighting pose of several species of big rattlers, with the anterior part of the body elevated well above the coil and the head drawn back. It not only rattled, it hissed loudly as well. Yet a few weeks later, I found an exceptionally big one that was utterly indifferent to my presence and was easily caught. On my next trip I saw a totally different looking rattler that seemed to be carved from pinkish brown granite. It was stretched full-length on a dense network of vines perhaps a foot above the ground. I didn't think I could pin it where it lay, so I grabbed it by the tail and flipped it onto solid ground. I got away with this maneuver, but I don't recommend it. This snake was a speckled rattlesnake, rarest of the three species in coastal southern California.

By carefully saving my gasoline coupons and trading duty periods with some of my friends, I was able to manage an overnight trip to the Borego Desert in eastern San Diego County. This area had recently become famous among herpetologists because of the ease with which interesting species of small desert reptiles could be collected by slowly driving the blacktop roads at night. Many of these snakes and lizards had previously been thought extremely rare, but by "running the road" it was sometimes possible to collect in one night as many specimens as had been in all the museums of the world prior to 1935. This is a good tactic that works not only in deserts but also in many other environments, if the season and weather are right and if the roads are not too wide and heavily traveled. I've tried it on three continents with fair to excellent results, although it is quite possible to spend half a night and put a great many miles on the car with nothing to show for it. My trip to the Borego was not a great success. With poor timing and inexperience, I found only a spotted night snake and a squashed sidewinder. Both were new species for me, but I'd hoped for much more. Nearly all the snakes I caught while stationed in San Diego were given to the zoo.

Many of the patients at San Diego Naval Hospital had filariasis or malaria. The former disease was almost unknown to American physicians. It is caused by an extremely slender roundworm that enters the body as a microscopic larva through the bite of a mosquito. In the form of the disease that we saw (Bancroftian filariasis), the worms mature in lymph nodes and their larvae circulate in the blood where they can be picked up by mosquitoes. The most dramatic complication of the disease is elephantiasis in which one leg or the scrotum enlarges to a grotesque and unbelievable size. Many medical texts of the time had an illustration of an unfortunate Polynesian with a scrotum the size of a bushel basket resting on a little cart. Some of the infected servicemen had seen deformities of this sort also. There was no treatment for filariasis at the time, and morale among the patients was not high. Many of our patients developed filarial fever during which the scrotum could swell to the size of a softball, but it always went down with rest and aspirin. What very few American physicians realized was that elephantiasis is uncommon even among heavily infected native populations, and almost always requires years of repeated infections. The most helpful and sensible thing the military did was to evacuate all infected personnel from the southwest Pacific and never send them back. None ever developed lasting deformity.

There were many patients with malaria, a disease that was still prevalent in parts of the United States. Physicians at New Albany regularly diagnosed it, although I do not know how often they were correct. My grandparents bought quinine in bulk, capsuled it on the kitchen table, and took the capsule for any illness with chills and fever.

Incidence of malaria was extremely high among military personnel in the Solomons and New Guinea. Atebrine was widely used as a suppressive, but it turned your skin yellow and there were rumors it caused impotence. Also, you didn't always remember to take it, particularly when people were shooting at you. Many of the patients at San Diego had been evacuated with a primary diagnosis of malaria, but others developed their illness following injuries or just happened to get sick while their ships were in port. Some types of malaria can remain latent for years. Malaria typically means intermittent chills and high fever, misery, and eventually debilitation, but some forms of the disease, particularly cerebral malaria, can kill very quickly.

More than one serviceman picked up by the police for violent or bizarre behavior and diagnosed as having a combat psychosis, was found dead a few hours later with the small blood vessels of his brain packed with malaria parasites.

Of course, San Diego Naval Hospital had many patients with less exotic illnesses and conditions. In the spring of 1943 we had a nasty epidemic of meningiococcic meningitis, particularly among recruits. Diagnosis of meningitis almost always requires a spinal puncture, not an easy thing to do on a disoriented, husky marine. Once, after I'd gotten the needle into the spinal canal and removed the obturator, the spinal fluid under greatly increased pressure squirted out and hit me in the eye. I went to my superior officer and told him what had happened. He put me on sulfadiazine for a few days, and I had no trouble.

In the summer of 1943 I saw penicillin given for the first time. I was on the dependents' service, and the patient was a young boy with staphylococcal septicemia secondary to osteomyelitis, a condition that was essentially a hundred percent fatal. The penicillin worked like magic; a few days later the youngster walked out of the hospital. A day or so later, we tried it on a girl with typhoid. As any first year medical student can tell you now, it had no effect. Penicillin was a great boon on the venereal disease wards, for gonorrhea was becoming increasingly resistant to sulfa drugs. At that time, any venereal disease was automatically misconduct unless you acquired it from your wife (I never knew a sailor ungallant enough to admit this), and it meant loss of pay and time toward promotion while you were on the sick list. While in the Navy, I diagnosed two cases of genital herpes. This infection was not recognized as being sexually transmitted at that time. I told the fellows they'd just acquired a cold sore in an unconventional anatomical site.

A month or so after I left for San Diego, Jacqueline Cochran recruited Madge for the newly organized Women's Army Service Pilots (WASP). In February, she left for basic training at Sweetwater, Texas. I was not very happy with her being in what I thought was a more dramatic arm of the service and getting her picture in *Life* magazine. Moreover I was afraid of losing her to some glamorous flyboy. I behaved very badly,

Madge in WASP training,
Sweetwater, Texas

and I'm surprised she didn't break our engagement. However, when she completed her training in August, she persuaded Miss Cochran to assign her to the Ferry Command base at Long Beach, California. From here she ferried military planes to nearly every part of the country. Long Beach is not very far from San Diego, but with our military duties and the restrictions on travel, our hours together were few and precious.

When she got to San Diego, we often would go to Tijuana. It may have been a tawdry border town, but to us it was a romantic place where gasoline and meat were unrationed. We had a favorite restaurant where we would order steak or venison and have a pousse-cafe, a drink in which several liqueurs of different colors and specific densities are layered one above the other. We were required to be back across the border by 10:00 p.m., so we had time for little else. On October 10, 1943, we were married. We each had five days leave. We had a proper church wedding, although

October 10, 1943

27

wartime travel restrictions prevented our families from attending. The only person linking us to our former lives was Madge's matron of honor, Ruth Murphy. Her husband, Ralph, had been a high school classmate of mine and a member of the neighborhood gang. He was in the Pacific with the marines. The others in the wedding party were Navy people. A fellow intern, Irvin Mattick, was best man. Our flower girl was Claire Holley. A few months before, I had been one of a surgical team that operated on her for a ruptured appendix, and I'd become a close friend of her parents. She was a lovely child. The day after our wedding, Madge and I headed down the coast of Baja California, stopping where the paved road did at the lazy little fishing village of Ensenada. The days we spent there were delightful—full of laughter and sensuality.

My year of internship soon drew to a close, and I was assigned to duty in the Pacific aboard the USS *Brooks*. Soon after Madge and I were engaged, we thought that Brooks would be a nice name for our first child—male or female. When I was assigned to a ship of that name, it seemed like an omen, a good one we hoped. One chilly winter day I left San Francisco aboard the Matson liner *Lurline* and eventually caught up with the *Brooks* at Milne Bay, New Guinea. The *Brooks* was an old destroyer commissioned the year I was born. She had been modified by removing her torpedo tubes and part of her engine plant to make room for additional personnel and boats to carry them. Her principal function was to carry small groups on quick and dangerous missions. With her guns and depth charges, she could also act as an escort if nothing better was available. She had a crew of about 150, and I was their doctor. A good many were members of a naval reserve unit from Burlington, Iowa. They were a healthy lot, and ordinarily I didn't have much to do. It is said that wartime sea duty is 90 percent boredom and 10 percent terror, and I have no reason to disagree. Aside from my medical duties, I was in charge of the wardroom mess which meant I got all the complaints about the food and had to arbitrate the racial problems of the black and Filipino stewards. As ship's librarian I had to explain why we got copies of *Black Beauty* instead of *God's Little Acre* from well-meaning ladies' clubs. I also stood a regular coding watch during which, in violation of a strict interpretation of the Geneva Convention, I deciphered messages sent to the ship.

I heard my first shots fired in anger at Hollandia in what is now West Irian. This port became a frequent stopping place for us, and I had a chance to see a little of the New Guinea jungle. Almost all the reptiles I saw were lizards—most of them I recognized as skinks. Once, a large head with forked tongue poked out of the undergrowth and I thought I had met a python, but it was a large monitor lizard. In the grassy country near Lake Sentani, I found on the trail what I thought was a most peculiar snake. It had a narrow head and long snout that suggested to me some of the tropical tree snakes illustrated in Ditmars' books, but it had no enlarged plates on its belly as a proper snake should. Much later I identified it as a pygopodid, one of a family of virtually limbless lizards found only in Australia and New Guinea. On another trip I found three human skeletons in a rock shelter near the beach. There was no military equipment nearby, so I assume they were unlucky natives caught in crossfire during a minor battle in the Pacific war. My shipmates found my lizard hunts amusing and gave me a decoration, the Order of the Silver Skink. An officer who saw me chasing a large green lizard up a palm tree near the officers' club on Manus Island shook his head and said, "They keep you guys out here too long."

I was largely ignorant of the many living things we saw while at sea. The luminous creatures fascinated me. They sparkled in our wake and flashed as we lay at anchor. I dipped them out and phosphorescence dripped from my fingers. On a coral beach I found some objects that looked like brightly banded sticks of chalk. I was sure they were aboriginal art objects, but years later learned they were spines of a sea urchin, probably a species of *Heterocentrotus*. Looking over the rail one day, I saw a huge gray object rise from the sea on our beam. I almost yelled, "Submarine!" before I realized it was a whale. Once I saw a turtle, and once the watch sighted a crocodile, but it had disappeared before I got on deck. Very rarely we saw a sea snake. From my reading, I thought the tropical Pacific would be full of them. Some thirty years later on another ship, I would be in these same waters hunting sea snakes. One of my shipmates would be a former pilot in the Imperial Japanese Navy.

The reality of war came home to me at Saipan in June 1944. We were carrying an underwater demolition team. Their job was to go in well in advance of a landing and clear away underwater obstacles of natural or man-made origin using explosives or anything else that was indicated. These teams were made up of skilled swimmers. There was no scuba gear. To qualify for the team you had to make a breath-hold dive of three minutes. Some of the team could do five. They were a prime target for whoever was defending the beach, and our team caught hell at Saipan. One man was hit by a mortar shell while in the boat. We buried most of him at sea; a bosun's mate scooped up the rest with one of the big metal helmets worn by talkers on the bridge. Two others were killed in the water and several injured.

Before dawn next day, Bob Milam, my cabin mate, shook me awake. "You better get up, doc. We got an unidentified contact on radar, and the old man's as nervous as a whore in church." The contact was a fishing boat abandoned by her crew. We boarded her, and I got some Japanese cigarettes and a phonograph record. During the height of the landing operations, we picked up wounded from wrecked amphibious vehicles and landing craft. It was a very busy time. One marine had a large piece blown out of his skull exposing the brain. I did the best I could, cleaning the wound and protecting it from infection. Some of the crew who saw this said their doctor could do brain surgery—the least deserved accolade I have ever received. Another marine had a shattered arm that I amputated. This was little more than cutting through some soft tissues and controlling bleeding. A few days later my pharmacist's mate said, "Doc, what did you do with that arm you amputated the other night?"

"Suffering Christ, I don't know! I think I threw it over the side."

"There's a hell of a smell down in the troop compartment, and I just thought I'd ask."

To my great relief, the smell came from a box of spoiled steaks.

Next day we were cruising close to the cliffs at the north end of Saipan. It was a lovely day, all was quiet, and I was on the flying bridge. Suddenly there was a flash of orange from the cliffs, and a column of water rose up to starboard. A few seconds later another flash and a column to port. If those Japanese were the gunners they seemed to be, the next shell should have landed on our bridge, but by then the old *Brooks* had begun a tight turn at her best speed, and the next salvo missed.

After the Saipan operation, the ship was ordered to San Francisco for refit. While I was at sea, Madge earned her instrument ratings in multi-engine planes at St. Joseph, Missouri, and took additional flight training in pursuit planes at Brownsville, Texas. Eventually she ferried ten types of military planes and had other flight experience with a half-dozen more. After my ship went into the Navy yard at San Francisco, I got two weeks leave to visit my family at New Albany. While I was there, Madge buzzed the town in a P-51 fighter. However, her favorite fighter was the P-47. When I returned to San Francisco, there was not much for me to do. Madge got leave and we had some wonderful days. We discovered Chinatown with its excellent food and Chinese art and craftsmanship. One late August morning we embraced, and I left again for the Pacific. The first letter I received from her had

Madge as a WASP during World War II

31

World War II

7 May 1944
My Darling Wife,

If I'm still all right when you get this, you can stop worrying about me, providing you've had any time to worry. We are soon to go back to civilization for several weeks at least, and I'll be safely holed up in a good liberty port. I don't want you to get any unwarranted hopes up, but there is a slight but definite chance I'll be seeing you in about six weeks. In any event, I'll soon be out of the war zone and will be out of it for a substantial length of time. We are lucky.

Beginning May 1st, I became Ward Room Mess Treasurer which means, among other things, that I am supposed to make spam, beans and potatoes look like a blue plate special. Suggestions will be appreciated.

There is a good sea running, and a trip to the beach in the small boat leaves us soaked to the skin but exhilarated.

While on the beach, I was surprised to see the familiar pages of the Indianapolis Sunday Star left on the wet sand by some unknown Hoosier.

I will see no spring this year except for the spring that goes on forever in our hearts. But if only I could see again the valley of the Ohio; only to see again the dear green hills! It is a long road.

Have had no letter from you in a long time. Mail reaches us so rarely here. I know you are writing; I know you are very near to me really. And soon we will live as free people again, forgetting the loneliness and the heat, the sameness of the days, the lonely, wasted nights.

And now, my Darling and always my Darling, I must leave you. "The long day wanes . . . . The Deep moans round with many voices." And perhaps it is not too late.

Je Reviens
Sherman

news that she was pregnant. I wasn't surprised. She had resigned from the WASPs and was living at home.

For a short time the *Brooks* did routine escort duty around New Guinea and the Admiralties. On one trip we were contacted by the submarine *Mingo*. She'd had some sort of mishap and couldn't submerge, so we saw her back to port. After she'd been repaired, her captain invited the *Brooks* officers to come along on a dive or two to see if the repairs had been successful. I'd been intrigued by submarines since I'd read Lowell Thomas' *Raiders of the Deep* as a schoolboy, so I eagerly volunteered. Compared with the *Brooks,* the submarine seemed clean, cool, and deadly efficient but even more crowded. Had it not been for the warning lights and sounds, I would hardly have known we were submerging. I'm sure the dive was a short and shallow one, but I can say I was on a working submarine in wartime.

In October we were alerted to prepare for the invasion of the Philippines. We sailed for Leyte and ran right into a typhoon. The hours of being slammed about in a rolling, pitching ship were as bad as combat. We developed a leak forward, and the evaporators that supplied our fresh water broke

Some of the crew on the USS *Brooks*. Sherman is the second from the left in the back row

down. One man hurt his leg badly, and I put on a cast, catching the bucket of plaster bandages as it slid by on the deck. In spite of this, we arrived at the beachhead at Leyte on schedule. We were luckier than at Saipan; I don't recall any casualties. On the ship's radio, we heard General Douglas MacArthur's "People of the Philippines, I have returned." speech. A few days after the decisive defeat of the Japanese Navy in the Battle of Leyte Gulf, the first suicide planes or kamikazes appeared. On our way to Mindoro, we saw the cruiser *Nashville* badly hit. She had carried MacArthur back to the Philippines, but I doubt if the suicide pilot knew this.

On New Year's eve 1944, several of us were in a small boat drinking beer (this evaded the regulation against drinking aboard ship) and watching the Japs bomb the beach. Soon after this, we left for Lingayen Gulf near the northern end of Luzon. This time we were part of a minesweeping operation. About noon on January 6, we were in the gulf, it was fairly quiet, and I was on deck. Then, over the coastal hills, came two dark green Jap Zeros. One streaked for the destroyer-minesweeper *Long* and hit her amidships sending up a great ball of smoke and flame; the other headed for us. I went down into the compartment where our little sick bay was. There was a loud clatter of bullets hitting the decks, a violent shock, and a great gust of hot air. Those of us in the compartment started up the ladder, but there was only fire at the top. We opened an emergency hatch and crawled out onto the main deck. The midships section was in flames, and a bomb had blown a great hole in the deck. This is where training and discipline pay off, because you're too scared and shaken to do any thinking. Captain Rasmussen, his face black and eyebrows singed, was leading a fire fighting party. Some men were throwing ready ammunition over the side; others were caring for wounded. Someone yelled, "Where's that crazy doctor!" Soon the big Australian destroyer *Warramunga* came alongside with fire fighters in asbestos suits on her decks. Many years later I talked to some of the *Warramunga's* crew, and they said they were terribly afraid we'd blow up and take them with us. But they kept their hoses going, and the fires were put out. I took our worst casualties, burns and shrapnel wounds, to *Warramunga* where

The USS *Brooks* after being hit by a Japanese Zero

her doctor and I worked for the rest of the day and most of the night. Periodically, the sound of her guns indicated more planes in the vicinity. Next day all the wounded were alive and they were transferred to the battleship *Pennsylvania.* I was given a short time to go back to the *Brooks* to pick up some personal belongings. We had lost eight men and our engines were wrecked. The ship never sailed again under her own power. Shortly after I got back to the *Pennsylvania,* I asked for my sea bag.

"Doc, it smelled awful strange, and we turned it over to the chemical warfare officer. We don't know what that Jap might have been carrying."

The explanation was simple. In the bag was a jar of lizards I'd picked up in New Guinea, Leyte, and Manus and preserved in formalin. The jar had broken in the transfer from one ship to another. I put the lizards in another jar, and they were eventually given to the San Diego Natural History Museum. Maybe they're still there.

By slow degrees the *Brooks* and her crew made their way back to the states. The ship was towed the whole distance, by

Sherman in Hawaii on the way back to California after the
Brooks had been destroyed

no means a cost-effective move, but I suppose the Navy hated
to write off a ship, however old and battered. During our stop
at Pearl Harbor, I learned I had a healthy daughter awaiting
my return. I was sent home on leave, and when I went back to
San Pedro, California, for the decommissioning of the ship,
Madge and our very small daughter soon followed. A few hours
before the *Brooks* flags were hauled down for the last time, an
infant who happened to have the same name had her formula
prepared in the wardroom. Not long after that, atomic bombs
annihilated Hiroshima and Nagasaki, and the war was over.

Soon after the ship was decommissioned, I received orders to
San Diego Naval Hospital and was assigned, at my request, to
the dependents' service. I thought this would be good preparation for a future career in family practice. Housing at that time
was terribly difficult to find, and we lived in some very margin-
al accommodations with Brooks sometimes sleeping in a bureau
drawer. In time we got a tiny but adequate house with a banana
plant near the back door. Soon after I got to San Diego, I called
the Holley family and learned that Claire was very ill with

rheumatic heart disease. She died a few days later.

My days at the hospital were heavy, and I saw some interesting cases. One was a young Navy wife who came to the hospital with a high fever, headache, and other indications of a severe but unlocalized infection. After about two days she was no better, so I started her on penicillin. A day or so later, she developed a rash. Thinking this a drug reaction, I stopped the penicillin. The same day, I got from the laboratory results of some serological tests I'd ordered. She had a strongly positive Weil-Felix reaction, which indicates a rickettsial infection such as Rocky Mountain spotted fever or typhus, and this also explained her rash. Her history pointed to murine typhus, an infection acquired from the bite of a flea that has fed on an infected rat. Like Madge, Brooks, and me, she was living in ramshackle housing where there were lots of rats. While she was still in the hospital, a second young woman with a very similar illness came to the clinic. This time I was alerted and made a diagnosis before the Weil-Felix reaction came back positive. This young woman lived in better housing but worked at a feed store where rats were numerous. Although there was no effective antibiotic for typhus at that time, both patients recovered. I reported the cases to public health authorities, but no one seemed to be interested.

About the time the ship was decommissioned, I became very depressed and unhappy and was drinking quite a bit. I had residual flashback reactions from combat and felt uncertain about my future. Neither a career in the Navy nor civilian practice seemed attractive. I found myself getting too much involved in the illnesses and troubles of some patients and being curt and impolite to others. Since medical student days, I'd occasionally taken barbiturates to relax and sleep; now I was taking them frequently and mixing them with Benzedrine. One especially bad afternoon, I took an overdose of barbiturate and woke up in the hospital. I don't think I intended to kill myself, but it was close enough. After some weeks hospitalization, the Navy thought I would be better off in civilian life, and in April 1946 I was back in Indiana. Madge, her parents, my parents, and my brother and sister all, in slightly different ways, stood by me through this very bad period.

World War II

Dear Dad,

It was strangely quiet that morning of 6 January 1945. For four days, air attacks had increased in frequency and intensity; and the preceding afternoon our task group had had a brush with two Jap destroyers sneaking out of Manila harbor. At dawn the sixth, a few snooper planes had been reported; but as the *Brooks* shoved her nose into Lingayen Gulf as the very first ship of the invasion armada, we might have been the only living persons in the world. Our task was to help in clearing the extensive minefields the Japs should have laid—but didn't—and to bring back any new type mines encountered.

Flights of white, egret-like birds drifted over the smooth water. Distant plumes of smoke still rose where our bombers had visited yesterday. Other minesweepers were in the gulf now, working methodically. All hands were kept at battle stations, but I forgot the war temporarily to watch a bright-colored sea snake swimming alongside as we picked our way through those potentially deadly waters at minimum speed.

At about 12:50, one of the sweeps reported she'd caught a mine; and we turned to investigate. About the same time, two enemy aircraft were picked up flying very low and just out of range. Suddenly they turned and streaked toward us. The Captain ordered them taken under fire and rang up flank speed. As I started down the ladder to sick bay, I saw the first plane crash into the destroyer-minesweep, *Long,* a few hundred yards on our starboard quarter.

I hit the deck at the foot of the ladder. As I did, there was a great blast of hot air; and the compartment was showered with sparks and singing fragments of metal. Of a dozen or so men in the adjacent troop spaces, five were hit, two badly. The compartments were filled with smoke; flames licked at the top of the ladder. Another chap and I opened an escape hatch, got ourselves and the other men topside.

The plane had circled and come in on the port side strafing all the way. Already afire, he'd rammed us just aft of number two stack and exploded. A 500-lb. bomb had blown a great hole in the deck and done lethal damage to our superannuated engines. Topside, the ship was bisected by a wall of flame and twisted wreckage. The forward engine room was flooding and all power gone.

This is it. This is where training and discipline pay off, kids, 'cause you're too scared and shaken to do any thinking. I emerged onto the well deck. The Captain, face black and eyebrows singed, was leading a fire fighting party. Al Hose was preparing to destroy his confidential publications and gear. Some of the men were throwing ready ammunition over the side; others were applying bandages or giving morphine to casualties; still others were just standing quietly like spectators at an automobile accident. One or two lost their heads and went over the side, but panic was quashed at its inception. No one knew what had happened to the men aft and no one asked.

Moments after we were hit, the big Tribal class destroyer, HMAS *Warramunga* nosed alongside us, her crew looking like strange monsters in their flame-proof hoods. Since our sick bay was untenable, I asked permission to take our most seriously wounded to the Australian ship.

From then until almost dawn, Surgeon-Lieutenant J. W. Begg and I worked over those men. We performed seven major operations, laying open jagged wounds to ligate hidden bleeders, remove fragments of bone and metal, restore some sort of anatomical continuity, pack in sulfa powder, and pray usually with mingled curses. We also had three bad burn cases that required plasma frequently. Every one of them pulled thru and many are already back to duty. But again I was forcefully reminded of the quotation from Ambrose Fare, "I treated their wounds; God healed them." But His job might have been made a little easier by sulfanilamides, plasma, and those boys' indomitable will to live.

For nearly two weeks after she'd been hit, the *Brooks* lay helpless and all but forgotten while the tide of the great Luzon invasion surged about her. An emergency generator furnished feeble, sporadic electric power. Cooking was done on one electric hot-plate and an improvised coffee urn heated by a blow torch. Portable gasoline pumps supplied fresh water and kept all compartments fairly dry except for the forward engine room where a large sea snake was reported swimming among the tangle of twisted pipes. Cushing says the snake was a reincarnation of the Jap pilot. It disappeared after terrorizing the entire ship. Nor was that the only terror. One night a fast motor launch slipped close by, and a lookout reported heaering Japanese voices in the darkness. Once an enemy bomber circled three times, then went off to seek a better target. Those on the ship feared each night the Japs would attempt to board her. They made up pass words and countersigns—for the first night they were: "Uncle Sam." "Because he got us into this mess." And for the second night: "Jesus Christ." "Because He's the only One that can get us out."

All the surviving crew members except six of the most seriously wounded rejoined the ship in Pearl Harbor for onward routing to the United States and new assignments. The old ship herself is bound for a west coast port and decommissioning or relegation to noncombatant duties.

It's wonderful to be back, but I feel my place is out with the Fleet. A few weeks visit with you all, Madge, and the little daughter; and I feel I should be going back out to help finish the job. Then I'll come sailing back for good.

Always,
Sherman

CHAPTER 3

HERPETOLOGY AND BIG BEND

I still had thoughts of practicing medicine in a small Indiana town, but I also had liberal education benefits under the G.I. Bill. Taking a year or so off and going back to school seemed attractive. My still strong interest in herpetology led me to the University of Michigan, one of the few places that offered training in that field. Although Blanchard was dead and Ruthven was president of the university, there was still an excellent group of Michigan herpetologists and a fine museum.

Ann Arbor was swamped with students in the autumn of 1946. Madge, Brooks, and I lived at Willow Village, a housing project built during the war for workers at the nearby Willow Run bomber factory. A few of the earlier occupants were still around, and one family lived next to us. Because the walls were literally paper-thin, we got a vivid and graphic account of their sexual and other shenanigans. They stole our coal, but otherwise we got on well enough.

Norman Hartweg and Charles F. Walker taught the herpetology course. Both were good teachers and great fun to work with. Under their instruction, I began to see herpetology as a scientific discipline rather than a sport. Jim Peters, a graduate student in the herpetology division, lived near us and we often drove to the campus together. His daughter, Jane Sara, was about Brooks' age, so Madge and Dorothy Peters sometimes exchanged baby-sitting duties. Other herpetology students included Charles C. Carpenter who was to do outstanding work on lizard and snake behavior, and Brahma Kaushiva from India. We invited him to our flat for dinner one evening, and

Madge did some rapid research on Hindu dietary customs, so we would not serve anything that might offend him.

I also took courses in the bacteriology department. Much of my work was under Dr. Walter Nungester who had been involved in some arcane mischief in biological warfare at Fort Detrick, Maryland. He also was an interesting teacher. I combined my interests by doing a small project on the venom of the Gila monster. There were two of these lizards at the museum and others at the Toledo Zoo, so I was able to get enough venom for my work. Nothing much came of it, but I learned something of the methodology of venom research. Near the end of the academic year, Nungester told me there was a position open in the newly formed department of microbiology at Indiana University School of Medicine. I applied for it, and in September 1947 I was back in the laboratories where I had been a student assistant five years before. Madge, Brooks, and I had a comfortable apartment in downtown Indianapolis.

From Ditmars' books, I learned there were wonderful snake dens near the southern tip of Illinois. In the spring of 1946, with my brother and Frank Powell, I tried to find them. As we headed south from Murphysboro, I looked to the east and saw a line of bluffs that looked like the Promised Land. And it was. Over the next few years, we visited it several times. I don't know of anyplace in the eastern United States that has a more interesting variety of amphibians and reptiles. It is a meeting ground for southern wetland, eastern forest, and western grassland species. Here I had my first experience with the venomous cottonmouth, which is one of the more plentiful snakes of the region. It's one of the few venomous snakes I've encountered that will sometimes stand its ground and fight when it has every chance to get away. The "stinging snake," a large black and red reptile, was known to all the local folk who were convinced it stung with its tail. Some said it would roll downhill like a hoop and stop itself by jabbing its tail into a tree that would immediately drop its leaves and die. Which once caused John to reply, "I suppose you must lose quite a bit of timber that way."

Hartweg and Walker told me that Indiana was a poorly known state herpetologically and needed an update of the only

44

previous study done by O.P. Hay in 1892. Now that I was likely to be in Indianapolis some time, this looked like a good long-term project. It was to be a major activity for the next seven years, and it's still going on. I've never had financial support from any organization, but a great many friends and colleagues, and a fair number of perfect strangers have helped out by permitting me to collect on their lands, contributing specimens, pulling my car out of mudholes, and occasionally offering a meal and lodging.

The herpetological year in Indiana begins with the first relatively mild rainy period of winter that brings salamanders to woodland ponds to breed. This can be as early as the first week of January. In the late 1940s I would drive up to 100 miles watching the roadside for suitable ponds. After dark, I stopped at the ponds and waded about looking for salamanders. Usually the first frogs were calling and their voices led me to other ponds. Inevitably I stepped into water over my boot tops or got soaked by rain. Well after midnight, I would get to bed wet and chilled to the bone.

Surprisingly enough, I didn't get pneumonia and I did learn something about the lives and loves of salamanders, particularly one called Jefferson's salamander. First I discovered that two species, which could fairly easily be distinguished in Indiana, were going under that name. Second, I confirmed an observation made by a Michigan zoologist in 1934 that some populations of these salamanders seem to be composed entirely of females. What was going on? Because salamanders of the all-female populations looked somewhat intermediate between the two species with normal sex ratios, I assumed they were hybrids, but this didn't explain the abnormal sex ratio. Tom Uzzell, then a University of Michigan graduate student, found the all-female populations had a triploid number of chromosomes that couldn't arise from ordinary sexual reproduction. Most salamanders have a curious compromise between external and internal fertilization. After various courtship rituals that may occur in the water or on land, the males deposit little packets of sperm, often on stalks. These are attached to the substrate or to objects such as twigs or grass stems. The females then pick up the sperm packets between the lips of their cloaca. So fertilization is internal without copulation. It now appears that the all-female populations of the Jefferson's salamander complex are sperm pirates that will pick up sperm from any of at least four species of salamanders. Ordinarily these sperm start development of the eggs but contribute nothing genetically, and the eggs produce essentially clones of the female that laid them. But rarely, because of water temperature and other reasons not fully understood, genuine hybrids are produced. What this will mean in terms of salamander evolution may be evident in another thousand years if there are any salamanders left.

I was by no means a full-time herpetologist, for my work at the medical school involved teaching, research, and a certain amount of diagnostic work. My first chief was Randall Thompson, a virologist. I have never liked viruses. They are made up of the molecules of life, but their form and behavior don't conform to other living things. They perceive nothing and carry on no metabolism. They have DNA or RNA but never both. They replicate only within living cells that they may or may not harm.

Dr. Thompson put me to work on a research project to try to find substances that would destroy viruses as the newly emerging antibiotics were destroying bacteria. Our chief model was vaccinia virus; the virus then used to immunize people against smallpox. We propagated it in eggs, animals, and a crude form of tissue culture, and tested various drugs for their power to inhibit it. We did find one group of drugs, the thiosemicarbazones, that were somewhat effective in inhibiting the virus. Eventually one of them was used in India as prophylaxis against smallpox, but a few years later smallpox was eradicated.

However, our interest in poxviruses led to involvement in a curious case. In the winter of 1951 a twelve-year-old girl living on a farm near Williamsport, Indiana, became ill with fever and a skin eruption. To her family physician, this didn't look quite like chickenpox; moreover, she'd had chickenpox. He called the state epidemiologist, Dr. J.W. Jackson. Dr. Jackson was an old-timer who had seen cases of smallpox; to him the girl's illness looked like alastrim, a mild form of smallpox. He collected material from pustules on her body, and from it Dr. Thompson and I isolated a virus undoubtedly of the smallpox group. Its source and exact identity remain a mystery. The girl had few contacts beyond her family and classmates, none of whom had a similar illness. None of the cows on the farm had a disease that might have been cowpox. Through a bit of good luck, she did not transmit her infection to anyone. During the time she would have been most infectious, Indiana was having one of its occasional blizzards and all schools in the area were closed. We called the microbe Williamsport virus and used it in some of our thiosemicarbazone work. When I left for Pakistan in 1958, there were tubes of Williamsport virus in the departmental freezer; they were gone when I returned.

Polio terrified everyone who had small children during summers in the late 1940s and early 1950s. Whenever one of our children developed fever, headache, and sore muscles, we crossed our fingers and prayed. Our lab was often asked to help in diagnosis of polio cases, but our very crude techniques were of little help. We tested many drugs against poliovirus, but nothing worked. The way polio was transmitted was unknown, however, its being a mostly summer disease suggested insects might be involved. Every summer we got curious insects sent to the lab with letters asking, "Is this the thing that is carrying polio?" We now know polio is one of the many diseases that are transmitted mainly by the fecal-oral route. Most children, particularly in lands where sanitation is poor, acquire mild infections and immunity early in life. When we went to Pakistan, sanitation had improved just enough that a few children were developing paralytic polio because they hadn't gotten infected quite young enough. Americans were blamed for bringing the disease to Pakistan.

In 1949 President Truman appointed my father to the Supreme Court, and he was one of the justices who took part in the landmark school desegregation decision. However, he was ill with coronary heart disease and pernicious anemia and resigned in 1956. He lived at New Albany in retirement until his death in 1965.

Our second daughter, Mary April, was born in 1951. While Madge was in labor, we calculated tibia-body length ratios for Indiana woodfrogs. I saw Mary April born; she was sturdy and

The Chicago Academy of Sciences

Founded in 1857 for the increase and diffusion of scientific knowledge
Lincoln Park - 2001 North Clark Street
Chicago 14, Illinois

Office of the Director

September 23, 1949

Dr. Sherman A. Minton, Jr.
Department of Microbiology
Indiana University Medical Center
Indianapolis 7, Indiana

Dear Dr. Minton:

Many thanks for your letter of September 15th, giving me the reference for the paper which appeared in Herpetologica. If Chapman Grant would ever get out two issues in the same typography one might be able to make an accurate guess in a similar situation!

The loan of specimens returned by you recently has been safely received although we have not yet had a chance to unpack the container. We shall send you at least a part of our series of crotalid snakes as soon as I (or Smith) can find an opportunity to pack them for shipment.

Even though it may seem somewhat out of order, I cannot resist asking if Justice Sherman Minton is a relative of yours. Is this question permissible?

Sincerely yours,

Howard K. Gloyd, Director

HKG:eq

handsome. Within an unexpectedly short time, Madge was pregnant again. One hot July night as we were sitting on our patio and she said, "I think I'm ready to have this baby."

"Nonsense, it's probably false labor."

"False labor, hell! We better get to the hospital!"

We just made it. A little later I saw Madge in her hospital room, "We've got another little girl."

"I'm glad. Does she have all her fingers and toes?"

"She does. I counted 'em."

And this was how Holly Susan arrived. I'm awfully glad we had our children before we knew of all the dreadful things your lifestyle and environment can do to the unborn. Madge didn't smoke and drank very temperately, but she took whatever medicines seemed to be indicated for the rare headaches and stomach upsets she had, and we were blissfully ignorant of all the pollutants industry was spilling into our air and water.

My friend Carl Gans once proposed a unit of time, the erp, measured in microseconds, between the time two herpetologists meet and the time they begin talking shop. This is why most of us look forward to meetings of the herpetological societies. The first one I attended was that of the Herpetologists League in 1948. This was a small society that was just getting back on its feet after having been dormant during the war. I also belonged to the American Society of Ichthyologists and Herpetologists that had a lineage going back to 1913 but was still a small group. Looking at the group photos from my early meetings, I can recognize nearly everyone who was there. The line between professionals and amateurs was indistinct. Nearly everyone was at least partially involved in field work, and meeting sites alternated between major museums and areas where there was good collecting. The field trip was always a high point. Progress of a hunting party across the landscape was something like Sherman's march to the sea.

One of the pleasures of herpetology has always lain in the interaction with other specialists and learning from their field experiences. Hence whenever Madge and Sherm were at a common meeting, I would try to join them for a field excursion, as they always performed some preliminary research regarding desirable sites both scenic and herpetological. Both their expertise and enthusiasm often proved attractive to local zoologists and herpetologists and consequently we were never lacking scholarly guides.

Wherever the meeting, the Mintons found interesting sites. I still remember Sherm expertly picking up copperheads in a Louisiana scrapyard while I was chasing down a series of small skinks in the adjacent scrub. Whenever he approached large and venomous beasts too closely, I was likely to be found chatting with Madge and admiring her latest purchases from a jewelry mart and receiving advice about bric-a-brac that Mabel might appreciate.

One rather spectacular meeting occurred during a venoms symposium in Tel Aviv, Israel. I had been appointed to chair a session and my mother was highly impressed, as the meeting photographs documented that the famous flea specialist, and scion of the Rothschild banking family, Miriam Rothschild, had been seated next to me. Several local herpetologists including the elderly Jacob Hoofien, bank manager by profession and herpetologist by avocation, had offered to take us collecting along the northern border of the country. As Hoofien was the coauthor of the handbook of local herpetofauna, we were thrilled at the promised experience. Some lizards and a snake had been gathered along the border road with Lebanon when Hoofien pointed to an impressive ruin in the distance and identified it as a long abandoned crusader castle. Cameras came out and another snake was approached when two camouflaged soldiers came out of the brush and started to scold Hoofien. Apparently the zone we had entered was protected and they were charged with assuring the safety of visitors. They did allow us to carry off the snake, of a species that I no longer remember, and it joined the collections the Mintons, later presented to the American Museum.

His medical background assured that Sherm was the consultant of choice for snakebite problems among those of us who were involved in research on the histology and biochemistry of venom glands. He belonged to a set of experts characterized by a profound streak of common sense and this led to several interesting discoveries. In 1971 a group of new Orleans biologists and physicians organized a symposium on the nature of snake venoms and issues of treatment In order to assure attendance from across the continent, they had the meeting take place during the carnival and had each group of visitors stay with local specialists. Thus, Mabel and I were the guests of mrs. Harold Fox. Various herpetologists arrived in uniforms. Findlay Russell wore a frog suit that permitted him to practice amplexus. Sherman climbed various light poles and waved at the occupants of the elegant floats, thus increasing our yield of doubloons and necklaces.

The most spectacular even occurred when a medical specialist was questioned about his treatment technique of radical debridement. I felt this to be rather severe treatment as it was likely to produce much scarring and other tissue damage. The response of "I am a surgeon, I Cut!" led to some interesting discussions in the audience. To me it documented the merit of studying the differences of treatment procedures offered by the diverse specialists. I decided that I would consult Sherm whenever any one of my students encountered snakebite problems.

Carl Gans

At my first meeting, I met Philip W. Smith, then a graduate student at the University of Illinois. We had somewhat similar backgrounds and very similar ideas about what we liked to do. Phil was beginning a herpetological survey of Illinois just as I was doing in Indiana. The projects complemented each other and we exchanged a great deal of information. He took me to herpetologically interesting areas in Illinois, and I took him to some of my favorite spots in Indiana. He was a superb field person with uncanny ability to look over terrain and tell what would be found there. He was as interested in small mammals as he was in amphibians and reptiles, and after he completed his herpetological survey of Illinois, he published an excellent book on the fishes of the state. Phil's wife, Dorothy, was a good naturalist, and they worked together much as Madge and I did. Phil introduced me to his major professor, Hobart M. Smith, whose *Handbook of Lizards* I'd used as a student at Michigan. Other graduate students in herpetology at Illinois then were Jim List, a quiet but very sharp Kentuckian, Max Hensley with a ribald, rustic sense of humor, and Les Burger, a demon collector. He would go anywhere and literally leave no stone unturned. Les' directions for reaching a collecting site might go like this: "Go down the dirt road 'til you come to a gate that says, 'No hunting or trespassing.' Walk down the wire fence that has a sign, 'Keep out, this means you.' Cut across the old field and you'll see a sign that says, 'Trespassers will be shot.' Duck under the electric fence, and there you are."

Roger Conant was one of my mentors in herpetology. He had written an excellent book on the reptiles of Ohio, collaborated with Dr. Clay in describing a new water snake from the Lake Erie islands, and was curator of reptiles at the Philadelphia Zoo. He helped greatly in getting me started on my Indiana project and incidentally involved me in the pursuit of a monster. We used to have monsters every summer in Indiana. Usually they were snakes that "were big around as a nail keg" or "left a track as wide as a truck tire." Sometimes they were four-footed beasts that roared, screamed, left huge pugmarks in the dirt, or made off with dogs or livestock, but the monster of 1949 was a turtle. Gale Harris, a farmer living near the town of Churubusco in the northeastern part of the state, looked over the waters of nearby Fulk's Lake and saw "what looked like a submarine on top of the water. When I looked closer, I saw it was a turtle." Later it was described as being as big as a dining room table, covered with moss, and weighing 500 pounds. In March the turtle eluded an improvised dredge and broke out of a ring of stakes that had been planted around it. By this time, catching the turtle had become a matter of community pride. A professional diver from Fort Wayne was engaged to attach a net to the behemoth, and an automobile wrecker was prepared to drag it ashore. The turtle took this round in a breeze when the diver's suit sprung a leak. About that time, the national press picked up the story. Roger Conant wrote asking me if I would try to verify the existence and identity of the turtle. My strategy was to use a face mask and snorkel (comparatively sophisticated equipment in Indiana in 1949) to locate the turtle. I had no illusions about my ability to drag even a forty-pound turtle out of the lake single-handed, but I hoped to dive down and hook a float on a thin, strong line to some part of the creature's anatomy so it could be tracked and captured. When I got to Fulk's Lake, I found its seven acres dotted with an assortment of traps, some of which looked capable of catching and holding a small submarine. A diver's rubber suit and metal helmet rested on a rough bench. It took about fifteen minutes for me to realize I wasn't going to be the hero of Churubusco either. The water was colder than I'd counted on and was the color of strong, murky coffee. There were enough waterweeds to hide an aircraft carrier. I spent the rest of the day swapping snake and turtle stories with the other hunters. By the end of summer, Mr. Harris' farm looked like the Sixth Armored Division had been holding maneuvers there, and the turtle was still at large. In a last, desperate move, an attempt was made to drain the lake. This created a wide margin of almost bottomless muck in which two turtle hunters became entrapped and nearly lost their lives. The "Beast of 'Busco" was never captured and lives in legend. Churubusco now calls itself "Turtle Town USA" and holds an annual Turtle Days festival.

The First International Conference on Venoms was sponsored by the American Association for the Advancement of Science as part of its annual meeting in Berkeley, California, in December 1954. Here I first met many scientists from nations around the world. Some I remember best were Paul Boquet of the Institute Pasteur in Paris, Chen-Yuan Lee from Taiwan, Erich Kaiser from Vienna, and Alistair Reid and Norman Corkill, physicians from outposts of the vanishing British Empire. Others like Karl Slotta and Heinz Fraenkel-Conrat had come recently to the United States from war-torn nations of Europe. Eleanor E. Buckley of Wyeth Laboratories was the principal organizer of the conference. Among the other Americans were Bruce Halstead, the Navy's expert on venomous marine creatures, Findlay Russell, an articulate young California physician studying stingray injuries, and Henry Parrish who had recently completed a nationwide survey of venomous animal injuries. From this group arose the International Society on Toxinology that now has some 600 members.

The most controversial issue of the 1954 meeting was cryotherapy, the treatment of venomous bites and stings by application of cold. Its chief proponent was Herbert L. Stahnke of Arizona State University. A world authority on scorpions, he had become involved in the treatment of their stings, although he was not a physician. He had found local application of cold quite effective. Unfortunately, he extrapolated this to treatment of snakebites. Opposed to him was Fredrick A. Shannon. He was a young physician who had studied herpetology under Hobart Smith at Illinois and was now practicing in Arizona. The two clashed in the bitterest exchange I have ever heard at a scientific meeting. Shannon was angry, witty, and acerbic, and had somewhat better scientific evidence on his side. Stahnke had the gravity of an established academic plus experience in speaking on radio and television. It was a stand-off, and the feud smoldered until Shannon died of a rattlesnake bite in 1965. For many years, cryotherapy continued to be used for snakebite and did more harm than good.

Madge ducked out of the meetings to pursue another of her interests, rock hunting. She rented a car and drove down the coast to Jade Cove near Big Sur. She returned with some handsome pieces of jade. After the meetings we went to Point Lobos where we heard sea lions calling from offshore rocks.

Herpetology and Big Bend

We then went inland into the redwoods where we were properly impressed by the size of the trees. Here we found some of the Pacific Coast salamanders and frogs.

In 1955 I was granted a sabbatical leave to visit the Big Bend country of Texas to study some of the infections that can be transmitted from wildlife to man such as bat rabies, Chagas disease, and some kinds of viral encephalitis. Early in February we left Indianapolis driving a jeep and a Packard station wagon loaded with household effects and field gear. While driving, we communicated by colored cards held against the windshield. This gave the kids something to do, however, all were wonderful travelers. Big Bend was pretty much a wilderness. The National Park was new and only partly developed. We lived a little off the park on the ranch of Olin Blanks of San Angelo, Texas. Mr. Blanks had once had sheep on the ranch but evidently found this unprofitable, and he only visited it occasionally with hunting parties. A Mexican-American family lived at the main ranch house as caretakers. We lived in a smaller cement block house near the abandoned sheep sheds and barn. We had electricity and our water was piped across the desert from a spring. The nearest town was eighty miles away. I took Brooks to the ranch house from which she rode twenty-seven miles in a pickup truck to a school on the park. Almost half her classmates were Mexican-American, and she soon picked up some Spanish. Her friendships led to an invitation to a Mexican wedding, which we recorded on 8-mm movie film. "Wetbacks" frequently crossed the Rio Grande and made their way through the rugged country to ranches where there might be temporary work. A building near our house was a common stopping place for them, but no one had told us. When the first ones wandered in, I took my rifle and walked out. "Is daddy gonna shoot those Mexicans?" asked April. I had no idea what to do, but they looked harmless and scared. In the future, we always left a few tins of food in the building.

Soon after we arrived, Brooks and I went down to the Rio Grande to look for mosquito and blackfly larvae. I pointed across the river. "Over there," I said, "is Mexico."

"Is that really another country?" she said in a quiet voice that meant she was terribly impressed. It was a country destined to be quite important in her future.

Our neighbors, the closest about three miles away, were typical of that section of the Southwest. Pat McKinney was a professional panther hunter. He brought us several skulls of those big cats and once a skin. Mr. Woodward found charging tourists to hunt agate on his land was more profitable than ranching. Maggie Smith subsidized groups of Mexicans that illegally collected wax plant (*Euphorbia antisyphlitica*) on the park. The wax from this plant had considerable commercial value. Mr. Gulihur and his sons had a ranch but were more interested in prospecting for gold. As is true of every part of the Southwest and Mexico, there were rumors of lost mines and hidden treasure.

Just south of our house rose the bare, boulder-covered slopes of the Rosillos Mountains. Beyond them were the Chisos Mountains, which rise to about 7800 feet and have forested slopes and grassy meadows. On the Rio Grande are three huge canyons, while smaller canyons, mesas, and desert flats spread over an immense area. There is a marvelous variety of wildlife in the Big Bend. On our first trip south from Marathon toward our new home, we saw three freshly killed bobcats spread-eagled on a wire fence. Coyotes were similarly displayed. I suppose this practice may stem from the custom of leaving the bodies of hanged criminals to warn others. I never saw a panther but twice saw tracks of one. Javalinas or peccaries were not uncommon. Once about twilight I found myself surrounded by a group of them. They appeared as quietly as shadows and just as quietly vanished a few moments later. In the early morning when Brooks and I drove from home to the ranch house, we saw badgers, ringtail cats, coyotes, and many jackrabbits. Camped one night by the river, I heard a loud splash as a tree cut by beavers fell into the stream. A big hog-nose skunk had a burrow under our house. Another skunk showed up dead in the spring that provided our water supply. Unfortunately, this was the day I'd taken a distinguished visitor to the spring to show him what a pure water source we had.

This spring was home for a colony of Trans-Pecos copperheads, at that time a very poorly known snake. Five species of rattlesnakes live in the Big Bend. Each morning Madge checked our yard before she let the younger children out to play. The commonest species near our house and the one we worried about most was the western diamondback. Diamondbacks in the Big Bend are not particularly big, one of four feet being exceptional. This is in contrast to some other parts of Texas where a rattler less than six feet is hardly worth mentioning, if you can believe the local folks. The Mojave rattlesnake looks very much like the western diamondback but averages smaller in size. It was much less plentiful; I took only one alive. Months later when I got the venom sample from this snake to the lab and injected it into mice, I got a shock. It was extremely toxic—much more so than venom of any North American snake I'd tested. Other workers, including Jim Glenn of Salt Lake City and my former student, Scott Weinstein, have shown that the lethal factor is a polypeptide called Mojave toxin found in venom of some, but not all, Mojave rattlesnake populations. It, or a very similar toxin, is in venoms of some other rattlesnakes.

Sherman in Big Bend, holding a blacktail rattlesnake, *Crotalus molossus*

In the mountainous, rocky areas, the blacktail rattler and mottled rock rattler were the species encountered. They were quiet snakes and usually easy to capture. The prairie rattler was the rarest species; we found just one, a roadkill.

There were other species of snakes in the region, many of them new to me. One of the most spectacular was the western coachwhip, which was bright pink and could be six feet long. These snakes were especially active after rain showers. Many of the rarest snakes were active only at night and were best hunted by driving the roads. Humidity seemed to bring them out. Madge and I used Holly's hair as an indicator. If it was curly, it was a good night to run the road; if it was straight, it wasn't worth the trouble. One morning I found a little tan snake that looked like its head and neck had been dipped in India ink. It didn't match any species known from the United States, so I gave it a name, *Tantilla cucullata* (from cucullus, the black hood old British judges donned when sentencing a prisoner to hang). Subsequently it's been shown that *cuculla-ta* is a subspecies of the Mexican *Tantilla rubra,* but my name still stands at a lower level in the taxonomic hierarchy. Current field guides call it the blackhood snake.

Big Bend also has a rich lizard fauna. Hardest to identify were the whiptail lizards of the genus *Cnemidophorus.* I counted five species in the region, and for one of them, the checkered whiptail, I had only females. Remembering Jefferson's salamanders in Indiana, I thought there might be a similar situation with these desert lizards. When I suggested this in a manuscript I submitted on Big Bend reptiles, the editors quite reasonably crossed it out, for I didn't have many specimens, and the odd sex distribution could have been pure chance. However, time and a lot of work by other people proved I was essentially correct. There are numerous all-female populations of whiptail lizards, including a second one in Big Bend that I didn't recognize. Moreover, all-female populations have subsequently been discovered in other families of lizards in various parts of the world. Some species engage in courtship and pseudocopulation; others occasionally mate with males of bisexual species. Feminism hasn't wholly taken over.

One morning as I was running my mammal trap lines, I saw a little antelope squirrel, apparently just out of the nest, lying beside a snap trap. The trap had missed killing him

58

UNIVERSITY OF ILLINOIS
DEPARTMENT OF ZOOLOGY
URBANA, ILLINOIS
U. S. A.

June 20, 1956

Dr. Sherman A. Minton
Department of Microbiology
Indiana University Medical Center
1100 W. Michigan Street
Indianapolis 7, Indiana

Dear Sherman:

      I dislike very much to see a big paper broken up unless it is absolutely necessary. How about keeping your Big Bend manuscript intact by publication in Ecological Monographs? If it is impossible to publish the thing as a unit, of course the publication in separate parts is the only possibility. I still hate to see it done, but I would do it myself if faced with the choice of splitting up a big thing or not getting it published at all.

      Since this is a matter of uncertainty and apparently will so remain for a while it is probably best that I return your manuscript. I am sorry things did not work out with Herpetologica. Good luck with the Lilly Foundation angle. It is a monstrous anachronism in our times that you should have to work so hard to get something published, in an era when there seems to be plenty of money for about everything else.

      The idea of tessellatus being a hybrid is certainly novel to me. It would explain certain facts, yet I am not by any means willing to regard the possibility as being too strong. The best information on habits I've found is in Strecker's paper on the Panhandle published around 1905. He records seeing females lay eggs, but he didn't describe any mating or courtship activity, and unfortunately failed to record the sexes of the specimens whose measurements he published! It is an odd situation and certainly worth further investigation and thought.

      Very sincerely,

Hobart

HMS:ab

Hobart M. Smith
Associate Professor
of Zoology

because he was so small but had stunned him. I dropped him in my pocket. When I got home, he had revived. We fed him milk from a doll bottle, and soon he was eating cereal, crackers, and almost anything else. Once he chewed the tails off four lizards I had preserved and was hardening in a tray. The girls named him Nutkin and he became quite tame. Each morning he ran over our beds until we were all awake. A short time before we left, a gust of wind blew a door shut on him and killed him. We also had a collared lizard, a kangaroo rat, and a Texas tortoise that wandered freely about the house, but none had the verve and friendliness of Nutkin.

We had a series of interesting guests come to our little house in the desert. Marlin Perkins, who then had a popular television show called *Zoo Parade,* came late in May. With him were John Werler of the San Antonio Zoo, Lear Grimmer of Lincoln Park Zoo, and Bern Bechtel, a young physician from Johnstown, Pennsylvania. Marlin had planned a segment of his show around reptile collecting in the Big Bend. It was very hot and dry, so most of the snakes were caught at night and recaptured next day for the camera. Lizards were more cooperative. We chased a brightly colored southwestern earless lizard right at Marlin who was filming. With one smooth movement, he bent down and caught it. About the same time, Karl P. Schmidt and two of his associates at the Field Museum, Dwight Davis and Hymen Marx, stopped by on the way back from a frustrating trip in Mexico. K.P. Schmidt already knew Big Bend; in fact, it was on his suggestion that we went there. He was a wonderful storyteller and each evening entertained us from supper well into the night. His fatal snakebite about two years later was virtually a death in the family for us.

Phil and Dorothy Smith and their daughter, April, arrived about the middle of June. A month or so earlier, Phil had solved a problem for me. I was running low on alcohol for preserving specimens. He had alcohol, but regulations made it impossible for him to ship it as such. So he filled a few jugs, put a small fish in each, and shipped the lot as preserved scientific specimens. Phil and I collected copperheads and other interesting reptiles in the Rosillos Mountains. Dr. Goethe Link and his wife and son came from Indianapolis about a month

Herpetology and Big Bend

Visitors in Big Bend: (from left to right) Sherman A. Minton, Hymen Marx, Dwight D. Davis, Karl P. Schmidt, Marlin Perkins, and John E. Werler

later. Dr. Link was a well-known surgeon, but he was also an astronomer and a very good naturalist, especially keen on hummingbirds. We showed him several interesting species. Winifred Moore, Ellen Comper, and Dorothy Blanchard were University of Michigan biologists chiefly interested in cacti—of which we had a nice assortment. Madge introduced them to agate hunting, and we played scrabble and argued philosophy.

While they were there, we left them in charge of the house and drove to Padre Island in extreme southern Texas. Here we camped among the dunes, played in the surf, and drove every evening to a small seafood restaurant that was one of the few permanent structures on the island. We caught a few of the essentially Mexican snakes and lizards that enter the United States in this region.

All of us stayed healthy but not the cars. Several times Madge left Brooks in charge while she set out to look for me as I walked homeward from a car immobilized by mechanical failure. Any but the simplest repair meant an eighty-mile tow to Marathon. Once I went into a very rugged area at dusk to set mammal traps. When I finished, it was black dark and I couldn't find the jeep. I did make my way to one of the park roads, and Madge picked me up about 2:00 a.m.

No doubt every old person looks back to a period in his life he would specially enjoy living over again. For me, it would be the six months in the Big Bend.

CHAPTER 4
COSTA RICA

In the summer of 1957 I went to Central America on a tropical medicine fellowship sponsored by Louisiana State University. Other Fellows were Everett Bracken (Vanderbilt University), Eli Chernin (Harvard), Emil Kotcher (University of Louisville), and Al Ritterson (University of Rochester). We spent about six weeks in Costa Rica with shorter periods in El Salvador and Guatemala.

Most of our work in Costa Rica was at the Hospital San Juan de Dios in San Jose under the supervision of Dr. Antonio Pena-Chivarria, an astute physician and a compassionate gentleman. Medical care in Costa Rica was good by Latin American standards of the day, although it was a bit startling to see two children occupying the same hospital bed at the same time. Parts of the hospital were more than a century old, and new wings and corridors had been added in marvelously haphazard fashion. There was a huge kitchen, very smoky and hot but quite clean. The food itself looked good, considering what the operating budget must have been.

We lived in the old but comfortable Pension Canada. The food included such delicacies as heart of palm soup and salad and many good local fruits and vegetables, although we got tired of fried bananas twice a day. We got pancakes for breakfast, but never more than one at the same time. One morning Chernin bawled at the waiter, "Dos pancakes zusammen!"

All of us spoke strange mixtures of languages. I had learned some Spanish from phonograph records before I left and could rip off stock phrases with a reasonably decent accent.

Unfortunately, I never got the answers that were on the records. Nevertheless, I was occasionally interpreter for the group. Kotcher's ploy when he didn't know the Spanish was to speak very loudly in French, for he had lived for a time in Indo-China. Chernin had lived in India and occasionally tossed in a few words of Hindi. The two of them would sometimes spend an evening trying to top each other's stories, leading Ritterson to comment that he felt like a small hamlet between Calcutta and Saigon. Generally our group got along well, but occasionally there were heated arguments. Kotcher once said to Ritterson, "Don't take that holier than thou attitude with me, Al!"

Ritterson replied, "But brother Emil, I am holier than thou."

Over the years, I've made several visits to Costa Rica and seen a good many changes. In 1957 the elaborately decorated oxcarts with solid wooden wheels were a common sight in the countryside. In 1993 they were about as common as Conestoga wagons in rural Indiana. In 1957 the Costa Rican agricultural worker made about $1 a day and lived a little better than a Big Bend Mexican. This has improved over the years. In 1957 one of our trips outside San Jose was interrupted by a minor traffic accident, causing Ritterson to comment, "Two cars on

Sherman and Madge in Costa Rica, 1993

this road today and we manage to have a collision." In 1993 on the road from Puntarenas to San Jose, Madge and I spent two hours in a huge traffic jam. In 1957 as I was riding a bus through the countryside, some coins slipped out of my pocket and lay on the seat. The boy sitting beside me called this to my attention. I believe this level of honesty hasn't changed much.

In 1957 the major medical problems of Costa Rica and the other Central American countries were intestinal parasites and malnutrition. Effects of the two reinforced each other. More than half the adults and about 90 percent of school children had at least one parasite; most had several. The big roundworm *Ascaris*, the bloodsucking hookworm, and the bizarre-shaped whipworm were found together so frequently local physicians referred to them as the trinity. All these worms lay eggs that are passed in the feces and undergo some degree of development in the soil. The warm, moist ground of Costa Rica was an ideal environment. In small numbers, none of these worms are especially dangerous, but enough hookworms will debilitate even a well-nourished person, and a mass of *Ascaris* can block the intestine. One child had so many of these worms that his intestines felt like pieces of rope through the thin wall of his belly. You had to be very careful in treating such children. Most of the anti-worm drugs then in use stimulated *Ascaris,* causing them to ball up with disastrous results. Piperazine citrate was the only safe and effective treatment.

Kwashiokor, or protein-calorie malnutrition, was a major problem in all the countries we visited, but particularly in El Salvador where there was a wide gap between the small, affluent upper class and the terribly impoverished majority. It was worse in the uplands, for the coastal people had a cheap source of protein in fish.

Chagas disease is prevalent in much of Latin America. Some believe that Charles Darwin became infected when in South America, and it accounted for his ill health in later life. It is caused by a protozoan that exists as a squirming, fishlike trypanosome in the blood and a nonmotile, but actively proliferating amastigote form in many tissues, but particularly in the heart. Many wild animals harbor the parasite. Armadillos and opossums are important in Central America. It is carried by bloodsucking triatomid bugs called chinches voladores or flying bedbugs in Central America and kissing bugs in the southern U.S. because they often bite on the face. This is one of the diseases we were looking for in Big Bend but did not find, although the triatomids were common enough that we got a few bites. I have seen these bugs as far north as southern Indiana. However, Chagas disease is not seen in the United States aside from an occasional case in south Texas. This is mainly because northern species of triatomids are constipated. Humans are nearly always infected when the bug defecates on the skin and deposits parasites—no defecation, no transmission.

We often went to rural health centers in the countries we visited, and this let us see something of the great natural diversity of Central America as well as the equally varied lifestyles and culture of the people. Returning from one trip with a driver who appeared to be about sixteen years old, the car's engine coughed and died on a long, heavily traveled hill just outside San Jose. Ignacio, our driver, got out and looked under the hood. The engine was still there, and his knowledge of automobiles apparently admitted but one other source of trouble. "Falta gasolina," he said. We tried to explain that cars didn't faltan with quite those symptoms, especially when the gauge still registered. We tried to persuade him to let one of us fiddle with the car, but he had apparently been instructed under pain of mortal sin not to turn the car keys over to Norteamericanos. It was getting dark and raining, so we hailed one of the little buglike Renault cabs, and Ignacio and Kotcher got in to go in search of gasoline. The Renault took off like a scorched mouse, zooming up the wet, dark hill in reverse. Traffic was brisk, but the little cab snaked through lanes of cars until it disappeared over the brow of the hill. In due time the cab returned, zipping around other cars and trucks with magnificent disdain for rules of the road but going forward this time. Ignacio and I poured the gasoline into the tank and soaked the sleeve of my shirt in doing so. By this time I wasn't sure Ignacio was aware of the inflammable nature of gasoline. "Por Dios, Ignacio," I said, "no cigarillos!"

He got into the car, stepped on the starter, and still nothing happened. It was clearly time for a coup d'etat, so Bracken said, "Permítame, por favor," and elbowed Ignacio out of the driver's seat. He got the car rolling and, just at the bottom of the hill, the engine caught. Ten minutes later we were at the Pension Canada.

About two weeks later, we spent three days at the ranch or finca of Max Cone, a wire-and-rawhide Norteamericano of the sort you'd expect to see on a frontier anywhere in the world. We flew down in his plane, a Cessna 170. For about ten minutes, he let me take the controls. He said I was a Chinese pilot—One Wing Low. Once on the ground, we rode horseback to school-houses where we held our clinics. It was not good medicine we did; it was more like handling casualties. Working from 8:00 a.m. until dark each day, we saw about 500 people. I hope we helped a few; I hope we didn't hurt any. It was hardest to turn away those with conditions we couldn't have helped even if we'd had the time and the drugs. At each site, one of us examined the patients and dispensed medication, another did microscopic examinations of fecal specimens, and a third kept records. The next day, we rotated. We saw many patients with intestinal par-asites, some children with whooping cough and measles, and a few cases of malaria. Skin infections were numerous. We saw a couple of patients with boil-like swellings that contained the plump maggot of *Dermatobia,* the human botfly (it parasitizes other animals as well). It has a very strange life cycle. The female fly, which is about the size of a large housefly, catches a bloodsucking arthropod, usually a large mosquito but sometimes a tick or deerfly, and glues her eggs to the belly of this insect. Next time the carrier takes a blood meal, the eggs hatch, and the tiny maggots enter the skin, often through the puncture made by the carrier. They grow just under the skin for several weeks, then emerge and drop to the ground where they pupate and com-plete their development into flies. Whenever I had a spare hour, I looked for reptiles and amphibians. Under rubbish, I found two caecilians. These are limbless amphibians resembling giant earthworms and not closely related to either frogs or salaman-ders. On a night hunt I saw two fiery red eyes as large as small marbles. They belonged to a giant frog crouched by a stump. As I grabbed him, he made an unearthly sound between a bark and a scream and kicked so strongly he got away. This was my introduction to the smoky jungle frog (*Leptodactylus pentadactylus*); later I caught another. Under a damp log, I found a peripatus, an oddity mentioned in zoology texts but seldom seen by zoologists. It is thought to be intermediate between worms and arthropods and looks like a velvety caterpillar. When I scooped it up, it ejected two jets of sticky fluid from openings near its mouth.

Costa Rica has one of the richest amphibian and reptile faunas of the world, and I have had only tantalizing glimpses of it. Along nearly every stream are basilisks, lizards up to about two feet long and lightly built. They jump off rocks or logs and run a short distance on the surface of the water without sinking. One species, usually seen in trees or bushes, is bright green with red eyes. Males have large crests on the head, back, and tail and are definitely the most spectacular lizards I have ever seen. In a city park in San Jose, I found small frogs that were light green above with undersides transparent as cellophane. Their internal organs were encased in a glistening white membrane. On the 1957 trip, I collected eleven snakes of ten different species. One was later described as a previously unrecognized subspecies. Only one, a coral snake, was venomous. When I caught a snake in the field, my colleagues would ask, 'What is it?"

I would reply, "I don't know what it is, but I know what it isn't." This was an arrogant and silly answer, for I had no idea how well some nonvenomous snakes mimic venomous species. Moreover, I didn't know then that the boundary between venomous and nonvenomous snakes is a tenuous one, but I was soon to learn. A few days before we left Costa Rica, I caught a bright green lora or parrot snake. I brought it back alive to Indianapolis and gave it to Bern Bechtel who was then a resident in dermatology at Marion County General Hospital. A few days later it bit him. Although it was a harmless snake by all accepted criteria, his hand swelled rather alarmingly for a short time. I was to discover this is not a unique situation.

There were nearly always snakebite cases at Hospital San Juan de Dios. Most were inflicted by a large pit viper known locally under about a half-dozen Spanish names of which the commonest were terciopelo (velvet one) or barba armarilla (yellow beard). Another species commonly implicated was the eyelash viper, so called because of the enlarged, pointed scales above each eye. This arboreal snake has many color varieties of which the most spectacular is a uniformly gold one known as oropel. Both these snakes seem to be more plentiful in cultivated land such as banana plantations. I heard of one unlucky worker who was bitten on the leg by a terciopelo and, as he went to seek help, grasped a vine and was bitten by an oropel. Patients who reached hospitals nearly always survived, although they sometimes had permanently damaged limbs.

In Guatemala and southern Mexico, a parasitic filarial worm with the rather euphonious name, *Onchocerca volvulus,* causes many cases of blindness. Like some other American tropical diseases, it is a legacy of the African slave trade. Humans are infected by the bite of a blackfly that injects a larval stage of the worm. The worms mature just under the skin where they become enclosed in firm, painless nodules about the size of a hickory nut. They produce microscopic larvae that do not get into the blood, but migrate more or less randomly through superficial tissues and are picked up by biting blackflies that continue the cycle. The larvae sensitize tissues to worm proteins, and this produces inflammation that can be destructive to the eyes. Inflammation of the skin may be severe and can mimic leprosy. The disease is characteristic of the mountainous coffee-growing districts, for blackflies breed in small, rapid streams. In 1957 the chief treatment was surgical excision of the nodules. This was done al fresco in the coffee plantations. Today there are effective antiparasite drugs, but the disease remains a significant problem.

CHAPTER 5

PAKISTAN

As a small child, some of my favorite stories were from Rudyard Kipling's *Jungle Books*. Mowgli, the boy reared by wolves, Sher Khan, the tiger, Bagherra, the black panther, and Kaa, the rock python were very real to me. Kipling's India seemed to me a magical place yet one I dreamed I would see someday.

It was 1958. As Madge and I drove back from a lecture I'd given at Lafayette, Indiana, the car skidded dangerously on the icy road. A January wind whipped thin snow across the windshield.

"Darling," I said, "that Pakistan project Hugh Headlee talked to me about is beginning to look better and better."

Dr. Headlee was professor of parasitology who had recently become coordinator of a program of postgraduate medical education between Indiana University School of Medicine and the government of Pakistan. When Pakistan became an independent nation, several new medical schools were established but they were terribly short of qualified teaching staff. This project would establish an institute providing instruction in the basic medical sciences for physicians whom would then teach in Pakistan's medical schools. Funds would come from the International Cooperation Administration, later to become the Agency for International Development. Dr. Headlee asked me if I would like to be the microbiologist. There was a nice tax-free raise in salary, good living quarters, and an adequate school. We heard negative things too: an abominable climate, culture shock, exasperating local bureaucracy, water shortages, and tropical diseases. However, I saw Headlee's pictures of

71

sand dunes and desert scrub that were bound to harbor snakes and lizards I'd never seen before. Madge thought of gemstones, handicrafts, and learning about a culture very different from ours. The girls were enthusiastic but with a few misgivings. Holly, remembering her experience with foreign language in Big Bend, asked, "Do we have to learn their Spanish?" After about five months of indoctrination, inoculations, and the thousand details that go with closing a house and preparing for a trip of at least two years, we left for Pakistan.

We arrived in Karachi in June. Although it was several hours after darkness, temperature and humidity were well in the 90s. Stepping out of the plane was like being enveloped in a vast, steamy towel. Madge had taken seriously what she'd read about standards of dress for women in Moslem countries and had been shaken up two days previously when Vatican guards told her politely that Brooks, who had just turned thirteen, was expected to observe the standards of dress of a woman rather than a child. Both left the plane wearing long-sleeve, high-neck sweaters. There was a long wait for our baggage followed by a mercifully short customs inspection. A little cool air was still trapped in our suitcases, and we let it flow over our hands feeling as a man stranded in the desert feels when the last water in his canteen trickles down his throat. The inspectors scribbled cryptic chalk marks on our luggage. A putty-colored lizard scooted across the ceiling and snapped up a moth. Our friends met us, steered us into waiting cars, and we began our drive into the city. Since nobody travels by day during this season if he can help it, the road was crowded with a motley collection of animals and vehicles moving with no discernible traffic regulations. The muggy air was soaked with the effluvium of miles of open sewers and a million domestic animals.

Americans working for U.S. projects in Pakistan lived very well by local standards. We shared a bungalow with another American family. In the Indian subcontinent, bungalow (bangla) implies an upper-class dwelling. We had air conditioning in every occupied bedroom, although it was of little help during the frequent power failures. We could purchase western style foods, liquor, and cigarettes at the U.S. commissary, but it was cheaper and often more convenient to buy food at the local markets. Also it was more interesting.

We had four full-time servants and four others who worked part-time. All were male and of varying degrees of reliability and honesty. One of our friends wrote, "Madge, did you know that in Indianapolis you were doing the work of eight men?" There was a rigid hierarchy of servants. At the top was the bearer. He directed the other servants, kept things running smoothly, and reported directly to me or Madge, the sahib and mem-sahib. Some bearers also did the cooking, but we usually had a cook who had some autonomy in his kitchen. He also did the marketing if asked. The hamal was a sort of apprentice bearer. At the bottom of the pecking order was the sweeper. He did the really dirty work. Part-time we had a mali or gardener, the darzee who did sewing, the dhobie who did laundry, and the chowkidor or night watchman. The bearer, the cook, and their families had quarters in our bungalow. In their own words, Madge and I were their mother and father. We were also their health care providers. Madge acted as midwife once and was in demand for treatment of eye infections where her tetracycline ointment generally worked wonders. I was more in demand for treating fevers and diarrhea.

Our first full-time servants were a bunch of rascals. Being Christians, they had no compunction about drinking our liquor. Thereafter I vowed we'd have only Moslems, and if anyone converted, he'd lose his job. Later we had excellent cook who ran a small gambling operation in his spare time. This brought a lot of strangers into the house including some who thought they'd been cheated. During our last year or so, our bearer was Hassan, a Pathan from the Northwest Frontier, as honest and loyal as a man can be.

There was no television in 1958, of course. Occasionally we would go to the local movie houses if there was a Hollywood film. The local films tended to be turgid historical dramas, and we did not understand Urdu well enough to get much out of them. But the girls wrote and acted in their own dramas. Scripts of some, "The Enemy Owl," "The Tiger," "The Ghost of Flaming Hall," survive. All the girls took lessons in Indian dancing and Brooks became very proficient. She earned a place in a dance troupe that gave performances throughout the nation including East

The Minton family, (left to right) April, Sherman, Holly,
Madge, and Brooks in her dance costume

Pakistan (now Bangladesh). A few Americans raised eyebrows
when her dance troupe was invited to the embassy of the USSR
to meet a group of Russian dancers.

Although there were other American physicians in our group,
I was the unofficial doctor for the local staff. This may have
been because infections made up so much of the illness we saw,
and I was the microbiologist. Sanitation was abysmally bad and
the municipal water supply was contaminated by sewage. Flies
swarmed and mosquitoes were common. Overcrowding made
transmission of infections from person to person very easy, and
malnutrition lowered resistance. When I saw a patient who was
seriously ill with high fever, I took a blood sample of about 10
cc. About half of this would go into culture media that would
pick up typhoid and some other generalized bacterial infections,

a few drops would be used for a malaria smear, and the rest would be used for serological tests. More often than not, I got an answer in time to begin some sort of treatment. When I went to Pakistan, Bern Bechtel said, "You're lucky. You're going where there are diseases you can cure." In 1958 most of the antibiotics and antimalarial drugs still were effective.

Cholera is supposed to be a classic disease of poor sanitation, but the picture isn't so simple. During the more than four years I was in Karachi, we had just two outbreaks of cholera. The first came a few weeks after I arrived and before our institute had much of its equipment. We were so short of microscope slides that we were cutting them from windowpanes. The cholera patients were not admitted to the hospital but were isolated in a large shamiyana rather like a circus tent. I wanted some material for future teaching, so I sent my technician for a fecal sample. He returned with a small jar containing what looked like slightly dirty water, but it had come from a patient, and a stained smear showed it contained innumerable cholera bacteria. The cholera organism looks like a short, slightly curved sausage and is technically known as a vibrio. There are many species of vibrios and some can be found in almost any natural collection of water, fresh or salt. A unique feature of the cholera vibrio is its ability to produce a toxin that causes a massive outflow of water and salts into the gut causing intense diarrhea and death from dehydration and salt loss. The amount of diarrhea and fluid loss with cholera can be twenty to thirty liters a day. Although it took centuries to realize it, cholera is very simple to treat—replace the lost salt and water. The trick is to include some glucose in the replacement fluid; otherwise it doesn't work. When we lived in Pakistan, we took a cholera shot every six months. We know now that the vaccine used then was next to worthless. Pakistanis said the best prevention was a hundred rupees in your pocket. For reasons not altogether clear the disease strikes hardest at the poor. The thing about cholera that interests me most is why it almost always comes in sudden local outbreaks that die down in a few months. Between outbreaks it is difficult to find the vibrios in the environment. When we were in Karachi, I sometimes told people, not wholly in jest, that the water was so filthy that the cholera vibrio, which is rather fastidious, couldn't survive in it. More seriously, I wonder if it stops making toxin and turns into a harmless water vibrio. Or goes into some unknown resting phase.

Malaria wasn't uncommon but too often it was the diagnosis for anyone with chills and fever. Few physicians made blood smears to confirm their clinical impression. As a matter of fact, it was not always easy to get a patient's permission to take a blood sample for any purpose. Most had a fear of losing any blood. When I saw the blood counts and hemoglobin levels of most of the population, this apprehension seemed not wholly unreasonable.

Among the chronic infections, tuberculosis was prevalent but often not diagnosed until far advanced. Streptomycin and isoniazide were readily available for treatment but often unwisely used. Thursday was the traditional day for lepers to beg in the Karachi bazaar. On other days, they stayed off the street. A German physician operated a small leprosy clinic near the center of Karachi. Occasionally I stained and examined slides from her patients. Many lepers were confined in the leprosarium at Mangho Pir about ten miles from the city. Here dust-colored hospital buildings are situated in an oasis with warm springs. The hospital was pitifully understaffed; in 1958 there was one physician, himself a leper. A pool in the oasis sheltered a small population of protected crocodiles that had been there more than a century. Madge and I went there occasionally to look at the crocodiles. We have written more about them in our book, *Giant Reptiles*.

Once the clinic sent a patient who seemed too acutely ill to have only leprosy. She had a discharge from her nose, and I made a slide from it. I didn't see any leprosy bacilli, but I saw great numbers of what appeared to be another sinister bacillus. I sent her back with a note, "This patient may or may not have leprosy, but I think she has nasal diphtheria."

Our microbiology laboratory at the Basic Medical Sciences Institute often did diagnostic procedures for adjacent Jinnah Central Hospital. This was a rich source of teaching material for us and for the pathology department. We also did diagnostic work for the U.S. Embassy physician. One afternoon I got a cotton swab and note: "Lesion on Colonel Numbat's finger. Please

Pakistan

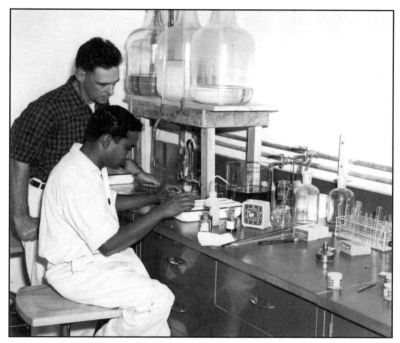

Sherman's laboratory in Pakistan

culture." I streaked the swab on our routine culture media and looked at the plates next morning. On them were some large, rough colonies like you might see if you cultured a pinch of soil from anywhere in the world. Under the microscope, I saw big brick-shaped bacilli in long chains. About then, the phone rang. "How about that culture from Colonel Numbat?"

"Doesn't look like much of anything unless, perchance, he has anthrax."

"That's exactly what I think he does have."

Inoculation of a guinea pig with the bacilli confirmed our impression. Anthrax in humans is a rare but very dangerous infection that can kill quickly. It's perennially toyed with in the context of a biological warfare agent. Luckily it is susceptible to penicillin. The colonel recovered, but he had a close call. A blood culture taken soon after my initial report was positive indicating his infection had become generalized. Anthrax spores can survive years, maybe a century, in the soil. It was our guess the colonel got infected while working in his garden.

During our last year in Karachi there was a major outbreak of smallpox. I visited the isolation hospital to collect some materials for teaching and saw dozens of cases including a few of hemorrhagic or black smallpox, which is invariably fatal and ghastly to see. All Americans and Europeans were urged to renew their vaccinations, and there were no cases among them. An American family got a bad scare when one of their children developed a bad case of chickenpox. Our lab was able to help with a quick, simple test that will usually distinguish the two infections. Smallpox is the only major infectious disease that has been eradicated by a massive, coordinated, international effort. An interesting question now is what to do with the last known tubes of the virus now in a very few presumably secure laboratories.

A world of new animals awaited us in Pakistan, although some were familiar from Kipling's stories. When I saw a little gray, sharp-nosed, furry creature scooting along a wall, I instantly recognized chuchundra, the musk shrew, who never has the courage to run into the middle of a room. The palm squirrel is a plentiful and friendly little animal that reminded us of squirrel Nutkin in Big Bend. House crows are cheeky birds that I have seen steal food from patients' trays on hospital verandahs. Pariah kites wheel and whistle, dodging telephone wires to pick up anything edible from the streets. They and several species of vultures were our unpaid scavenger service. Other city birds we soon learned to recognize were mynahs, hoopoes, bulbuls, and bee-eaters. We shared our house with two species of geckos, and a half-dozen other kinds of lizards appeared on the outside walls and shrubbery. During the monsoon, Indus toads called incessantly from rainpools, and later their newly transformed young were so plentiful you could hardly avoid stepping on them. A few weeks after we arrived, I had a call that a snake had been killed on the grounds of the American Embassy and would I please identify it. I quickly located a copy of Malcolm Smith's snake volume in the *Fauna of British India* and keyed out the reptile to the ganma snake (*Boiga trigonata*), a semiarboreal, slightly venomous species that was fairly common within the city. Over the next four years, we got numerous requests to identify snakes killed in city and suburban gardens. If killed by a servant, the snake's head was usually crushed to a pulp, something that detracted from its value as a museum specimen. Dick Zweifel, curator at the American Museum of Natural History once wrote me, "Do you ride around on an elephant trained to squash the heads of rare snakes?" When I asked why so much violence was needed to kill a snake, I was told the reptile's eyes had to be destroyed. If not, its mate might see in the dead snake's eyes the image of the person that killed it and take appropriate revenge.

The commonest snake around Karachi and in most parts of Pakistan is unfortunately the most dangerous. This is the saw-scaled viper, which gets its name from the sawtooth ridges on its lateral scales. When the snake is alarmed, it inflates its body with air and rubs the loops against each other. This makes a sound like water sprayed on hot coals. It has several local names; commonest in the Karachi district were "loondee," "afee," and "khuppur." Kipling calls it "karait" in several stories. Unfortunately the krait of herpetologists is a totally different serpent. The saw-scaled viper is a small snake rarely reaching a length of two feet. Its colors blend well with the desert soil, but it lives in other habitats including villages and cultivated fields. It eats almost any creature it can swallow. It is a most irritable snake, very quick to strike, and it will sometimes move toward a person who disturbs it. Its venom has unusually high toxicity for humans. It acts chiefly by destroying the clotting power of the blood and damaging small blood vessels. This action is prolonged, and a person may die of internal hemorrhages a week or two after he is bitten. Evidence indicates saw-scaled vipers cause most of the snakebite fatalities in Pakistan.

After our car arrived, we had more mobility and began to explore the countryside. The technique of running the roads at night that works so well for reptile collectors in the southwestern United States was also effective in Pakistan, but one limiting factor was a paucity of suitable roads. Just one major blacktop road connected Karachi with the rest of the nation. However about ten miles from our house was an area known

LIFE, LOVE, AND REPTILES

THE AMERICAN MUSEUM OF NATURAL HISTORY
CENTRAL PARK WEST AT 79TH STREET
NEW YORK 24, N. Y.

DEPARTMENT OF AMPHIBIANS AND REPTILES
CHARLES M. BOGERT, A.M., Chairman and Curator

RICHARD G. ZWEIFEL, Ph.D., Assistant Curator
THERESA A. CURTIN, B.A., Scientific Assistant
JOHN A. MOORE, Ph.D., Research Associate
ROGER CONANT, Research Associate

ARCHIE F. CARR, Jr., Ph.D., Research Associate
HERNDON G. DOWLING, Ph.D., Reseach Associate
SAMUEL B. McDOWELL, Ph.D., Research Associate
SHERMAN A. MINTON, Jr., M.D., Research Associat

August 20, 1959

Dr. Sherman A. Minton, Jr.
BMSI/USOM
American Embassy
A.P.O. 271
New York, N. Y.

Dear Sherman:

Here is the belated list of identifications on your last shipment, with our catalog numbers following your numbers in parentheses.
As you no doubt know, several of the specimens represent species not
previously sent by you: Psammophis schokari, Eumeces schneideri,
Spalerosophis diadema, Eublapharis macularius, Kachuga tectum, Varanus griseus, Spalerosophis arenarius and Ablepharus grayanus. The
last two were not even represented in the AMNH collection. S. arenarius, if correctly identified, is quite rare. Hy Marx recently re-
viewed the genus and had to settle for three literature records for
the species.

Not on the list is No. 82004, the "new" turtle. Sam McDowell's latest version of this is that it is Hardella indi Gray, based
on a single skull and left in the synonymy of H. thurji since time
immemorial. He still thinks it may represent a new genus, and in
any event it is a very good find. Sure hope you can get some with
locality data.

Along the lines of your inability to find any males among
your specimens of Cnemidophorus tessellatus, some Russians have just
reported a subspecies of Lacerta that consists wholly of females re-
producing parthenogenetically. If we can accept the work and trans-
lation, it looks as if they have eliminated all reasonable alterna-
tives to parthenogenesis. I suspect this will trigger a burst of investigation of Cnemidophorus for the same phenomenon. Curiously, the
report is that the parthenogenetic Lacerta hybridizes with populations
with normal reproduction.

Best regards,

Richard G. Zweifel

RGZ-ms
encl.

as the Malir Cantonment. In the British days, it had been a major military base and had a network of narrow but fairly good roads. Part of it was still used by the Pakistani army, but traffic was light. It was flat semidesert with dense clumps of "tor," a large, cactuslike euphorbia and "uk," a giant milkweed. For a short time during and after the monsoon, grass would carpet the ground with a deceptive coat of green. Crossing the area were several large gullies or nullahs with a few straggly trees clinging to their banks. These nullahs were usually dry but could become raging torrents after heavy rain.

A most interesting reptile that we encountered on an early night trip was the fat-tailed or leopard gecko. In 1958 very few herpetologists had seen one of these lizards alive. To the desert people, it was the hun-khun, a mysterious and terrible reptile whose bite was more deadly than that of a cobra. It could safely be killed only by blows with a leafy branch, because a drop of its blood falling on the skin was fatal. It is a rather stocky lizard that reaches a length of about a foot. Strictly nocturnal and slow for a lizard, it conducts a spirited defense when cornered. Rising high on its legs, it arches its back and waves its tail rather like a scorpion preparing to sting. It opens its mouth and makes a sound like air going out of a small balloon. It will bite, but is completely nonvenomous. They were abundant on the cantonment. My friend, Jerry Anderson, a professional animal collector, got about seventy one night. I was annoyed with him and made some remarks about killing the proverbial goose. Jerry sold most of his reptiles to dealers in Europe, but some of his geckos were reaching the U.S. in 1962. The leopard gecko breeds readily in captivity, is easy to keep, and lives a long time. Today it is a standard item in the reptile pet trade.

When clumps of the big euphorbia die, they collapse and form a low mound of dead branches. This traps a bit of moisture and provides shelter for a variety of creatures including small lizards and snakes. Here I found a tiny and distinctive gecko that was sulphur yellow with broad, dark crossbands. Although it was plentiful, it belonged to a genus never previously reported from the Indian subcontinent. Steve Anderson, Jerry Anderson, and I eventually gave it a name, *Tropiocolotes persicus euphorbiacola,* which was longer than the lizard.

I met Sherman for the first time at the ASIH meetings in Vancouver, BC, in 1963. I was a first-year grad student at Stanford that year, and beginning to write my dissertation on lizards of Iran. Sherman had recently returned from Pakistan and had with him the manuscript for his book-length study of the amphibians and reptiles of Pakistan. I had wandered into someone's room where drinks were going around, and Sherman was talking with Joe Tihen, as I remember. After introductions, Sherman and I began talking about the herpetology of Southwest Asia, and I had found another mentor.

We only encountered one another at meetings over the next 35 years or so, but I sought his advice by mail from time to time, and he peer-reviewed a number of my papers. His treatise on Pakistan herpetology was always a model for my own work. He was always generous with his helpful advice and comments. As a result of his continuing interest in Pakistan, we were often working on similar projects, and we published one paper on geckos of Southwest Asia together with our mutual friend, Jerry Anderson, who resides in Pakistan.

In 1989 or 1990, Kraig Adler approached Al Leviton about republishing *Khalaf's Reptiles of Iraq,* timely for the Gulf War. Al suggested a new work of larger scope, since he and I were working on a more general herpetology of all of Southwest Asia, and Kraig wisely brought in Sherman as a coauthor on the project. Sherman's treatment of the venomous snakes and snakebite made the book far more useful to military operations in the region. Unfortunately, the book was not published until after the war was ended. Nonetheless, it is frequently cited by workers on the fauna of Southwest Asia, even though some jokingly call it "The Herpetology of Desert Storm."

I regret that I never had the opportunity to work in the field with the Mintons or to know them better. As is often the case with people we respect, I waited too long to convey my gratitude for Sherman's friendship and collegiality, which had meant a great deal to me over a long period.

Steve Anderson

Pakistan

Saw-scaled vipers were common on the cantonment. Their presence in the euphorbia mounds along with some dangerous scorpions made hunting in this habitat quite challenging. Another relatively common snake was the Indian sand boa. It is a stocky snake up to a yard or so in length. If it is well nourished, its tail is about the same size and shape as its head. Local people believe it has a head at each end, one functioning during the rainy season and the other during the dry season. Metaphorically they are right; the thick, stubby tail stores fat to nourish the snake in times when food is scarce. The tail is also used in defense. When the snake is alarmed, it coils with its tail exposed and head hidden. One night I found a sand boa coiled in the open with its tail torn and bleeding. Tracks indicated it had been attacked by a fox or small jackal. Its injuries were trivial and healed in a few days.

For Madge and me, Malir Cantonment will always be associated with hedgehogs. The more attractive species was the small-foot hedgehog which was grizzled white and gray, and about the size of a croquet ball right out of *Alice in Wonderland*. The Indian hedgehog was a bit bigger, with larger ears and was predominantly black. Nearly all the hedgehogs we found were on the road at night. They were easy to catch. When they rolled up, they would puff and make hunching movements as though trying to punch you with their spines. They were uncomfortable to pick up with bare hands but not nearly as formidable as a porcupine. They did well in captivity and we sent several to the Philadelphia Zoo. Hedgehogs are said to be enemies of snakes, particularly vipers. A Pakistani family we knew asked us to give them a hedgehog to protect their home against snakes. We found no evidence this belief is true other than once seeing a hedgehog eating a road-killed saw-scaled viper.

We saw other animals also; jackals were common here, as they are almost everywhere in Pakistan. Occasionally we saw desert foxes and small wildcats not much bigger than house cats. Gerbils were common and burrowed around bushes. I dug one out and we kept it for many months. Occasionally we saw the Sind hare, which is a little smaller than a jackrabbit. The local people hunted it for food.

When Madge and I went back to Pakistan in 1984, Malir Cantonment as we knew it was almost gone. Expansion of the city and construction of a major highway had nearly destroyed it. There are probably a few leopard geckos left, and any animals that adapt to buildings and trash piles will doubtless be there until the remote future.

I learned of cobras early in life from Kipling's *Rikki-tikki-tavi,* a story of a brave mongoose that defends a British family living in India from a pair of particularly villainous reptiles. "Cobra" simply means snake in Portuguese, and some English-speaking Pakistanis used it in that sense. One of our servants woke me one morning announcing, "One of your cobras is loose!" I had no cobras at the house, and the escapee was a quite innocuous reptile. Herpetologists use the term for snakes of the genus *Naja* plus a few other species that are similar in appearance. Cobras in my old natural history books always had their hoods spread. With the hood lowered—the normal state so far as the snake is concerned—they are rather ordinary looking serpents. Once when I was visiting behind the scenes in San Diego Zoo, I saw a nondescript little snake in a two-gallon glass jar. I'd begun to unscrew the lid when Si Perkins said, "You know, of course, that's a young cobra."

We'd been in Karachi more than a year before I saw a live cobra in the wild. The snake charmers had them, but when I asked where the cobras came from, I got only vague or evasive answers. When the Basic Medical Sciences Institute really got rolling, I started a program of research on snake venoms and offered a price of ten rupees (about $2) for cobras. Within a very short time, I had about a dozen and promise of as many more as I wanted. Eventually I learned the best country for cobras is the grassland of the Indus Delta. They were found around the edges of Karachi but not often. One hot day during the monsoon season, three employees of the Institute came to my office. They had just been to a rubbish dump to dispose of some dead dogs and other refuse from the laboratories.

"Sahib, we have seen a very big snake!"

"As long as a man!"

"Oh, much longer!"

"Perhaps the sahib would be catching this snake?"

Pakistan

I wasn't interested. The dump was a miserable, malodorous place; moreover snakes seldom stay around after they've been spotted. One of the men was Daniel, an animal caretaker who helped me with the captive snakes in the lab. I gave him the Pilstrom snake tongs and a large bag and wished him luck. In a short time, the three came back with wide grins and a bag holding a large and handsome cobra. It was a few inches over five feet and very plump and sleek. We named it Sumitra for the Rani of Jhansi who fought against the British during the Indian Mutiny. It lived in the lab more than a year and gave the greatest single yield of venom I have ever obtained from a cobra, 610 mg dry weight. Eventually it was given to the Philadelphia Zoo.

After seeing how timid cobras are in the field and how much of their defense, even when cornered, seems to be bluff, I wondered how they could take even a fraction of the human lives they are accused of taking. From Sumitra I learned part of the reason. She had a hiding box—something essential for the well-being of most captive snakes, particularly nervous species like cobras. She soon became quite defensive when in the box, darting her head out in a disconcerting manner when the cage was opened. Years later in the snake room Madge and I had at Indiana University Medical School, we had a Chinese cobra that was much more assertive. At the least disturbance, it would lunge out of its box and rush to the glass front of the cage. If the cage was opened, it would dart its head about with its mouth slightly open. I suspect that most people who are bitten by cobras (snake handlers excluded) have disturbed the snake in some refuge where it felt secure. I heard of many fatal cobra bites and saw a few that were not fatal, however there was a strong tendency to ascribe all snakebites to cobras.

Another deadly snake we found in Karachi was the Indian or blue krait. This is a vividly marked black and white snake usually about a yard long. It adapts well to living in city gardens and rural villages. It is strongly nocturnal and sometimes, for unknown reasons, bites sleeping persons. The bite is not painful but is often followed by respiratory distress. Some rural folk believe the snake sucks the breath of sleepers, and if the person is not allowed to see daylight, he will recover. By day, kraits are very quiet and inoffensive. The wolf snake is a

Whenever he was free from his medical duties, Sherman Minton was in the field in West Pakistan. His chief objective was to become familiar with the herpetological fauna of the country. He did a lot of collecting and, with the help of Madge, his beloved wife, and their three daughters, he kept a living menagerie. Periodically, when he returned on leave to the United States, his diplomatic pouch contained an abundance of herpetological livestock which he distributed to friends. Much of it came to the Philadelphia Zoo and I had a big advantage over other recipients. I could estimate the fair market value of the live animals and send him a letter stating he had given specimens worth so many dollars to the zoo. It served as a deduction from his personal income tax each year.

Because we were building up our collection of photographs, my late wife, Isabelle Hunt Conant, and I took pictures of virtually every species he sent to us for the zoo. Thus, when he published papers (*An Annotated Key to the Amphibians and Reptiles of Sind and Las Bela, West Pakistan,* AMNH Novitates, No. 2081, and *A Contribution to the Herpetology of West Pakistan,* AMNH Bulletin, No. 134), we were able to lend him prints from our personal collection. When the various specimens died at the zoo, I preserved and then deposited them in the AMNH collection.

Roger Conant

harmless mimic of the krait. One afternoon, a snake charmer stopped at the house with reptiles to sell and found Madge sitting on the verandah. After the usual greetings, he pulled out a small black and white snake. "Sangchul?" said Madge, using the local name for the krait.

"Sangchul nay," said the snake charmer putting the snake in her hands. About then I stepped out onto the verandah. "Drop it!" I said, "It's a krait."

I've often wondered what the snake charmer had in mind. I'm quite sure he knew the snake was a krait. Perhaps he was testing Madge's knowledge of snakes, or maybe he wanted to see if she was immune to venom.

I'm sure some of the local people thought we had magic power over snakes. Once Madge and I captured a large non-venomous snake superficially similar to a cobra before the amazed eyes of two Baluchi goatherds. They pointed at the lapis rings we wore and clearly indicated that they thought these were the source of our magic.

A major family recreation was going to the beach. All our girls were good swimmers. At one of our beaches was a reef where we saw interesting sea creatures such as starfish, octopi, colorful nudibranchs, and sea hares that expelled royal purple dye. We didn't see any sharks and heard of no shark attacks. Occasionally swimmers were stung by the blue-bottle which is similar to the Portuguese man-of-war common on Florida beaches. Several species of venomous sea snakes are found near Karachi, but we rarely saw one at our beaches. Occasionally people brought us one found stranded and dead or dying. On a night road-running trip, Madge and I found one on the road near a brackish creek. It was a species that never leaves the water voluntarily, so we assumed it had been dragged or dropped onto the road by some predator. I bought many sea snakes from commercial fishermen. Although they were mortally afraid of some perfectly innocuous lizards, they thought the snakes practically harmless. "If they bite, rub with salt. Everything will be alright." The beaked sea snake, the one they caught most often, has caused numerous fatalities in Malaysia and Thailand.

In the late summer and fall, the big attraction at the beach

15 January 1959

Dear Roger:

You and Malcolm Smith just don't know anything about the snakes of Pakistan. Last weekend Madge and I were guests of one of the Pirs who are both religious leaders and big landholders in the rural parts of the country. Our host lives in and rules a village in the Indus Valley about 160 miles northeast of Karachi. He regaled us with tales of sundry herpetological wonders to be found in his territory such as a type of viper with hair on its head, a small deadly snake that flies into pieces when struck, a snake with a mouth at each end, a small snake that can jump from the sand and strike a man on a galloping horse, and other prodigies. On the more conservative side, he described a snake "with pattern like a carpet" that grew large enough to eat hares (does Python molurus reach the lower Indus?). He also said that the number of deaths from snakebite in the district where he lived (about the size of the largest midwestern counties and densely populated), "might be no less than one hundred annually." He described vomiting of blood as a prominent symptom of snakebite, so I suspect Echis is the chief culprit in his domain. Madge and I did not see so much as a frog or lizard during our visit, but the weather was rather cool. We were told that snakes were most plentiful during the summer and early autumn floods.

Our weather the past month or so has been delightfully cool during days and downright chilly at night with occasional light rains. Except for Gymnodactylus and a few other small lizards that are fairly common under sun warmed slabs of rock, the collecting has been poor. Gardners have contributed a couple of Typhlops, and the commercial fishermen got me a nice series of Enhydrina schistosa. It is interesting that the fishermen show no particular fear of this supposedly very poisonous species.

I'll try to get together some kodachromes of the more interesting herpetofauna for you, but it may be some time. Phil and Bernie Bechtel have gotten all my duplicates, and I had the misfortune to lose two of the last three rolls I've sent back to the states for processing.

Best wishes to you and Isabelle,

Sherman

Kindly provided by Roger Conant, to whom it was written

Pakistan

was watching the sea turtles nest. Nearly every night, huge gray-green female turtles lurched onto the beach, dug holes in the sand, and laid about a hundred eggs. Once a turtle had started her nest hole, nothing short of dynamite would move her. She would literally lay eggs in your hand. Because of religious proscriptions, the local people did not eat the turtles or their eggs. We breakfasted on the eggs a time or two finding them good but not exceptional. As the eggs hatched, little turtles by the hundreds erupted from the sand. Very few survived the multitude of predators that awaited them.

Eventually we traveled over much of Pakistan by automobile, mostly in our jeep station wagon. Karachi is at the southwestern edge of the province of Sind. Much of Sind lies in the lower valley of the Indus River and some of its tributaries, and is essentially a huge oasis. On both sides is desert, flat to the east and increasingly hilly to the west until you reach the formidable Kirthar Range. To the north is the Punjab, land of the five rivers and the best agricultural land in that part of Asia, with wheat the principal crop. However, it also has arid and mountainous areas. In the northernmost part of Pakistan are the Himalayas. On trips into the little semi-independent state of Swat, we could see snow-covered peaks more than 20,000 feet high. Baluchistan is the western part of Pakistan and is a vast region of inhospitable desert and mountains. There is a saying, "Merciful Allah, having made hell, why was it necessary to make Baluchistan?" However, all these regions have centuries of human history behind them and were sites of civilizations far older than Greece or Rome.

Roads varied from good, although never more than two lanes wide, to impassible without low-range four-wheel drive. Since the smaller water courses were dry most of the time, bridges were a luxury. When rains did come, you looked at the flow of water across the road and took your chances or waited until the water went down. Fuel supplies were chancy. Many villages had gas pumps, but sometimes had no gasoline. In a pinch, you could occasionally flag down a truck and buy a gallon or two from the driver. We usually carried a jerrycan of gasoline and one of water.

The rest house or dak bangla was the equivalent of a motel. These had been built in the days of the British Raj for use by

89

Sherman in the Sind Desert, holding a monitor (*Varanus*)

Pakistan

Madge helping Sherman photograph a lizard in Baluchistan

government officials traveling on official business, but in our time they were available on a first come, first served basis unless someone very important wanted a room. Some were quite comfortable, others were literally falling into ruins. A staff of one to a half-dozen servants would tidy up, provide security, and cook your meals if you wished. There were charpais or roped beds on which you put your bedroll or sleeping bag. Bathing and sanitary facilities were generally primitive. If there was no rest house or hotel, you camped. Sometimes this was the better option.

When I was stopped at military checkpoints and asked to show identification or if I stayed more than a day or two in a village, word would get out that I was a doctor and I would be asked for medicine. I carried an extra supply of aspirin, soda mints, and vitamin pills that I felt I could dispense without doing any harm. In one remote Sindhi village I was asked to see a woman, in itself an unusual request. She had what appeared to be an advanced cancer of the lower jaw or possibly an infection such as actinomycosis. I gave her all but two of my Demerol tablets, a box of moist, scented towelettes, and several rupees with a request that she be taken by train or bus to the nearest hospital—a pathetic and useless gesture but all I could offer.

Most of our herpetological specimens went to the American Museum of Natural History, so we were in frequent contact with Charles Bogert, then curator of reptiles. In 1959 he wrote, "This will serve to introduce Dr. Walter Fairservis. Perhaps you can be of service to Walter in view of your knowledge and experienced gained in Karachi . . . Walter is one of the more enlightened archeologists who is willing to take the time to preserve and document amphibians and reptiles when he encounters them. He sent us some extraordinarily interesting material from Afghanistan . . ."

Walter arrived in November and was our houseguest four months. He was specially interested in civilizations that flourished in southern Baluchistan some four thousand years ago. However, his first problem was to get his jeep and some other equipment out of customs. This took about two months. Fortunately for him, we had transportation and field gear. He reciprocated with some wonderful entertainment and companionship. He was unquestionably the most erudite baby-sitter our children ever had.

Walter's first trips with us were into the district of Las Bela which is west of Karachi across a little river today called the Hab but which Alexander the Great knew as the Arabius. The oddly Spanish-sounding name of the region means "forest of the Lassi," an ancient displaced Sindhi tribe. Today the forest is reduced to a few small remnants. Las Bela consists of a long strip of arid coastline with valleys extending inland from it. These are flanked by steep, barren mountains that for most of the year reflect heat into the lowland like a vast solar oven. Temperatures of 115°F in the shade aren't unusual in summer; I recorded 106°F at sundown in June. Little rivers from the north draw ragged lines of green down their valleys and even within the hills scattered springs well up, each one nurturing a small island of vegetation.

In the widest of these valleys where some agriculture is possible, is the city of Bela. It is the Rambacia of Alexander; even in his time it must have been very old. Madge, Walter, and I first went there in the last week of 1959. Most of the Karachi-Bela road was a track winding through powdery dust and bottomless sand. I remember the relief we felt when we finally climbed onto the hard talus fans. It was rough but better than the sand that kept us plowing along in the jeep's most powerful four-wheel drive and the dust that turned our faces into clay masks.

To enter Bela was to leave behind the twentieth century. For most of the local people, it was life without electricity, piped water, and internal combustion engines. The people themselves were a mixed lot. This is the only place in Pakistan where I saw many persons with distinctly African features and dress. Their presence is attributed to the Arab slave trade. Many others had dark skins but Aryan features of the sort that can be seen from the Indus to Isfahan. Occasionally you saw a Pathan with fair skin and pale eyes.

The last day of the year saw us about ten miles north of Bela on the bank of the Porali River, a little intermittently flowing stream. Walter had read that some miles to the west were numerous caves cut into cliffs along the Kud River, another little desert stream. We thought we could get no closer to them by jeep, so we set out on foot. Hardly had we crossed the Porali when we began literally stumbling over low stone walls. Walter picked up some broken bits of pottery and shouted, "My God, it's a site! And a big one!"

However, the caves were still our goal. We hiked off across the rocky desert and reached them about midafternoon. They were impressive but seemed disappointingly free of artifacts. After searching for an hour or so, we started back. Darkness fell long before we got to the jeep. "Head for the belt of Orion," said Walter, looking at the starry desert sky. Before we got back, we blundered into an encampment of Baluchi nomads who were already asleep. Murmuring, "Asalaam alaikum" to prostrate forms, we trudged on. A bit later, we fell to our knees in a sandy nullah. Temporarily too weak to go on, we lay on the sand and sang "Auld Lang Syne." When we finally reached the jeep, we had to put up the tent and unroll our sleeping bags. We had just enough energy to drink a bottle of champagne.

Next day we went to the site just across the Porali River. It was indeed the remains of a fair-sized city that had been baking under the desert sun for hundreds of years without attracting an archaeologist's attention. Walter named it "Edith Shahr" (City of Light) and has described it in his book, *The Roots of Ancient India* and elsewhere.

In February a U.S. Navy oceanographic survey ship put in at Karachi. Madge and the girls visited the ship and invited the helicopter pilots to dinner at our house. During the evening, she suggested that the pilots might have an interesting flight and incidentally advance the cause of archaeology by flying up the valleys of the Porali and Kud Rivers. They made two flights with Walter and Madge and discovered a whole complex of previously unknown villages. Near the Kud River caves was a clear pool of water that looked like a fine place to swim, so they set the helicopter down on a sandbar. Nearby, the holy man who lived in one of the caves was praying. I doubt if he'd seen a helicopter before much less had one land virtually at his front door; nevertheless, he calmly finished his prayers. On this trip, Madge caught a most curious lizard, the blunt-tailed spider gecko, which always looks like it's at the point of starvation.

We visited this part of Las Bela several times during the next two years, usually taking with us other folk who were interested in archaeology such as George and Barbara Dales of the University of Pennsylvania, Jane Bunting whose husband was deputy director of the U.S. Agency for International Development, and Major Robert Brewer, a U.S. military adviser. We found it was possible to drive much closer to the Kud River caves. The artifacts we picked up cut across times and cultures. There were Harappan figurines of mother goddesses and bulls, painted pots of the Nal culture of northern Baluchistan, Parthian spouts, bronze spearpoints, and stone cannonballs of the Islamic invaders. The animals we encountered were also a queer mix. A gazelle might be nibbling grass beside a pool where a crocodile floated, the dainty footprints of a desert fox might cross the lumbering track of a pangolin, and an Indian garden lizard could look down from a tamarisk branch and see a remote relative from the Arabian desert. One night as we were camped on the Hab River, we heard unearthly laughing sounds. "The villagers are trying to frighten us," said Madge.

Pakistan

I knew the sound from an earlier trip with Walter. "Not villagers," I said, "hyenas."

Next morning, April walked to the river's edge and frightened a crocodile into the water. Generally we did not find many reptiles on these trips but they often were unusual ones. I caught a second and very rare species of spider gecko one night near the Kud River caves.

We became well acquainted with Jam Mohammad, the Nazim or political administrator of Bela, and he was a generous and helpful host. He invited us to an Eid feast celebrating one of the major Moslem holidays. The main dish was goat roasted on stakes around an open fire. On the way to Bela, I caught a large specimen of the uncommon red-spotted snake, and my handling it at the feast gave me something of a reputation as a magician among the guests. This is not altogether comfortable, because you may be expected to sustain it.

Jam Mohammad told me that if I wanted many snakes, I must come to Bela during the rainy season. So in mid-September I drove to Bela with Jerry Anderson and his wife, Lauretta. Jerry is a Scotsman who had lived a long time in Pakistan and was an enthusiastic field naturalist and good company. It was dark when we reached the city, and we camped in the Burra Bagh or Big Garden, which is well outside. Here, probably on an oasis, the Jams or rulers of Las Bela when it was an independent state had planted banyans and other trees to make a refuge from the merciless sun. Tombs of the Jams lie in the garden. We pitched our tent among the trees and began hunting. The buttressed trunks of the banyans were alive with geckos, most of them the common and widely distributed Indian house gecko and the Persian gecko with a few bark geckos tossed in for variety. Snakes were represented by several of the unpleasantly ubiquitous saw-scaled vipers, a beautiful little wolf snake, and a kukri snake, a small snake that feeds largely on reptile eggs. More hunting in the hours just after sunrise added more species. Of the fifteen or so reptile species I collected on the Burra Bagh, more than half seemed restricted to it and a few other oases and were never taken in the surrounding desert. It is hard to say if these are natural relict species or species accidentally introduced by man.

North of Bela the road is a rocky track winding up the Porali River into the mountains. After twenty miles or so, we came to a ford at the base of a steep hill. The river itself looked passable, but at the bottom of the hill the primitive roadbed was gone, leaving a base of large sharp boulders. We'd already changed one tire and our gasoline was low. The noon sun was making an inferno of the rocky bluffs, but along the river was shade from scrubby tamarisks, and on the bluff above was an abandoned mud and thatch house. It looked like a good place to stop. The house was bearable enough despite residual scents of previous occupants. We dozed through the afternoon, rousing occasionally to go down and soak in the river. Toward evening we heard the unfamiliar sound of an automobile engine. Down the hill inched a big truck piled with bedding and merchandise with about a dozen Baluchis sitting on the load. The truck bucked and lurched perilously as it hit the boulders. At the edge of the water, it stopped. There was grinding of gears and racing of the engine, then the driver and his helper got out to inspect the damage.

"Kia bat hai?" (What's the matter?), I yelled down at the driver. He shouted back something like, "ek saal, ek saal!" In Urdu this means "one year" and made very little sense in context, although it just might have been a fair estimate of the time needed to get the truck back in running shape. Jerry, who is proficient in the local languages, smiled thinly as he usually did when I tried to converse in any of them.

"He's trying to answer in English. Translate 'ek saal' as 'axle'. He also wants to know if you will take him back to Bela."

"Not today. Tomorrow morning."

"That's all right. The people will camp here tonight."

As the sun set, heavy black clouds gathered around the mountains to the north and lightning flickered about the peaks. The head man of the Baluchis came to our camp.

"Rain is coming. This river is dangerous as a snake. Much water will come down from the mountains. Can your jeep pull the truck from the river?"

It had begun to shower briskly as we rigged a towing cable from the jeep to the truck. On reasonably level ground we might have been able to pull it, but on a steep, rough slope it was hopeless, even with most of the people pushing the truck. One man climbed to the top of a large rock and began to chant, beseeching aid from all the Pirs and Imams of Baluchistan. The truck didn't budge, but presently the rain stopped and a bright moon appeared. It seemed as if his message had gotten through to headquarters. We lighted our lanterns and set out to look for reptiles. It was not a very productive hunt, although we got one snake and five geckos belonging to as many genera.

About midnight we spread our bedding along the bluff. The rain had freshened the air but also brought many fiercely biting sandflies out of crevices. Beneath the moonlight the landscape had a silky sheen, but the sound of the river grew loud and deep. I looked toward the ford. The truck lay on its side in a millrace of muddy water with petrol drums and bales of cloth bobbing beside it.

"Flash flood!" I yelled, and soon both camps were awake, but there was nothing we could do. The full force of the water caught the truck and rolled it over and over. The wooden sides popped; metal ground and crunched against rock. Within an hour, the truck had vanished completely. When morning came, we saw two wheels sticking out of the brown torrent about a quarter-mile downstream.

We lost little time starting back to Bela, for we had no idea what the rain had done to the road. As it turned out, there was no deep water or serious damage. In the city, we arranged with Jam Mohammad to have help sent to the people stranded on the riverbank. We strolled through the covered bazaar and stopped at Jam Mohammad's bungalow where we had tea and nibbled at hunks of a sweet, gummy local confection. It was past noon when we were again rolling toward Karachi. The afternoon heat had begun to weaken as we passed through the village of Uthal into grass and sparse acacia scrub. Jerry and Lauretta dozed in the back seat. Suddenly the largest cobra I have ever seen in the field glided across the road. I stopped, jumped out, and raced to cut off the snake's line of escape. It spread its hood and rose in a fighting pose with its head almost as high as my waist. Jerry was out of the car almost at once and clamped the snake tongs onto its body. Lauretta hunted frantically for a second pair of tongs. When we had them, it was comparatively easy to work the cobra into a bag. A few days later, I killed and preserved it, for we needed a voucher specimen for the Bela region. It was a few inches short of six feet long.

One of the world's oldest civilizations arose in the Indus valley some four thousand years ago and is known as the Harappan civilization from Harappa, one of its larger cities. However, its largest and best preserved city is Mohenjo Daro, which is about 170 miles (airline) northeast of Karachi. By road or train, it is considerably farther. Brooks, Holly, and I went there in the autumn of 1958 with two American nurses; April was ill, and Madge stayed in Karachi with her. The British archeologist Stuart Piggott conveyed our first impression when he wrote, "The secrecy of those blank brick walls, the unadorned architecture, the monotonous regularity of the streets, the stifling weight of dead tradition combine to make the Harappan civilization one of the least attractive of ancient Oriental history."

The wood needed for kilns that baked those brick destroyed the primordial gallery forest along the Indus. Ancient Harappan art shows rhinoceros, elephants, and tigers, animals that thrive in extensive grasslands and have vanished from the mixture of semidesert and cultivated fields that we saw in 1958. Centuries of irrigation have had a devastating effect in some places. To quote Piggott again, "In the dreary country around Larkana, the soil is so impregnated with salt that . . . it has a brittle shining crust that crushes beneath the step like a satanic mockery of snow."

Overgrazing and hunting have eliminated most of the large wildlife, but our nurse companions were bird watchers, and they added to their life lists some new species such as the pheasant-tailed jacana and the fishing eagle. As a herpetologist, I was frustrated by seeing dozens of basking turtles that I couldn't catch or identify.

There is one area where some hint of the Indus valley of Harappan times can be seen. This is the region around Manchar Lake where I made several visits in search of herpetological specimens. In the dawn hours of November 6 I lay in my sleeping bag and listened to the sound of wings of tens of thousands of birds. Most were migratory ducks, terns, sandpipers, whimbrels, and storks; others were resident species. The lake and surrounding canals held several interesting turtle species seldom seen by western naturalists, and I got one glimpse of a crocodile. The lake people were friendly and helped me catch turtles. The women who poled the boats had little of the shyness so typical of village women in Pakistan.

We sometimes felt we were maintaining a guesthouse for archeologists, but all were delightful people. Samuel Noah Kramer and his wife Millie spent several days with us. Dr. Kramer was the leading authority on Sumerian culture, and he had come to Pakistan to try to decipher the Harappan picture-writing. He had no better luck than anyone else, but I think he had fun. We went with them to the Indus valley site of Amri where a French party headed by Dr. and Mrs. Casal were carrying out excavations. While we were with the Casals' expedition, I helped by identifying turtle shell fragments, but what impressed them most was my striking kitchen matches with my thumbnail, an old cowboy trick the French evidently hadn't seen. During their digging they uncovered a tiny snake about six inches long, pale pink, no thicker than the lead in a pencil, and with head and tail the same size. It was one of the thread snakes (*Leptotyphlops*) a widely distributed family whose Asian members are poorly known.

The city of Tatta lies near the western edge of the Indus Delta. During its days of greatness in the fourteenth and fifteenth centuries, it stood on the banks of the river, and the first European visitors described it as a city larger than London. When we first saw Tatta, it was a crumbling shell of a town with only the great Mosque of Shah Jahan and the thousands of stone tombs on Makli Ridge testifying to its vanished glory. It is also home to the Jogis of Sind, the snake charmers we came to know well. The snake charmer has been part of the westerner's image of India since the days of the first European trading companies. But he goes back far in time and deep into the culture of his land.

Tatta is the hub of the Jogi world. The life of the tribe revolves around the capturing and displaying of snakes. The best showmen go with their baskets and flutes to Karachi and other cities where they may spend several days wandering about and giving performances, particularly in the better class neighborhoods. Some snake charmers remain in the cities near hotels and railroad stations where they can readily attract an audience. They replenish their stock of snakes by barter or purchase from their country cousins.

The traditional show with flute and cobra is simply an exploitation of the cobra's natural defensive behavior. The show usually begins with the Jogi blowing into the snake basket and rapping it on the ground. He then lifts the lid and the cobra rises to perhaps a third of its length with its hood spread. The snake man or his partner now begins to play his flute, swaying his body as he plays. The snake also sways, following the man's movement rather than the music. Cobras used in shows are rendered harmless by breaking off their fangs and cauterizing the sockets or by sewing the mouth shut. This severely limits the life of a cobra in show business but is a wise precaution. One afternoon we were watching a snake show while a monkey-wallah and his simian companion waited in the wings hoping to profit from an audience already on the spot. Suddenly the monkey darted into the circle of spectators, seized a cobra by the tail, and flipped it into the crowd. There was instant panic but the defanged snake could hurt no one.

Jogi snake charmers in Pakistan

Pakistan

Other snakes are regularly used. Pythons contribute little to the action but their size makes them good attention getters. Saw-scaled vipers with their peculiar crablike movement and vicious striking make an interesting attraction. The Indian sand boa with its plump, stubby tail is often billed as a two-headed snake. Jogis may mutilate the tail to simulate eyes and a mouth. Large harmless snakes such as the dhaman and royal snake are often used, for they put up an impressive fight and few know they are not dangerous. A cobra-mongoose combat may be part of the performance. Rarely does either principal have any heart for battle, and it usually develops into a real farce with the cobra doing its best to escape and the mongoose sulking or going into a hysterical screaming fit. Eventually the animals may be goaded into a fight of sorts. If the crowd is sufficiently bloodthirsty and prosperous looking, the mongoose may be allowed to kill the cobra or a harmless snake may be substituted. The audience is expected to pay the snake charmer handsomely for the loss of his snake.

A snake charmer expects to pick up fees occasionally for ridding a house or compound of snakes. If there aren't enough resident reptiles, he is not above planting a snake or two on the premises and capturing it before the amazed householder. Sometimes they are lucky, as a 1971 newspaper story goes: "Weddings always bring problems. For the marriage of Pakistan president's son in Karachi last week there was the need to flush the cobras out of the garden. The task required the blandishments of eight snake charmers. Three cobras were captured, one of them eleven feet long." If the length of that cobra was correct, it couldn't have been native to Karachi.

Jogis have a reputation for knowing magic, both black and white, and sell charms, the most potent being the small gold crown worn by a hundred-year-old white cobra. Another potent talisman is the "mun," a luminous stone some cobras carry in their mouth to light their way. We were not privileged to see either of these marvels, but we did see several snake stones that are applied to snakebites to extract or neutralize the venom. Most were rough agate cabochons or bezoar stones that come from stomachs of goats or other animals. Recently we have heard that some of the younger Jogis now use and

Sherman with some of the Jogis

deal in drugs. I was very sorry to hear this and a bit surprised. Charas and bhang, both cannabis preparations, were available in Karachi in the years we lived in Pakistan but were not used or supplied by Jogis.

Jogi women are not veiled, but they are kept sequestered from eyes of strange males and do not permit themselves to be photographed. The older women may be sent out to beg. Quite early during our stay in Karachi, there came to our gate an old woman carrying a skinny, half-grown python and leading a small girl. Jogis show great affection for their younger children, and the youngsters themselves are generally plump and healthy looking. Not many see the inside of a schoolroom, but their lot seemed to us better than that of children in the Karachi slums.

We spent enough time in the field with Jogis to learn something of their hunting methods. We saw them use no technique unknown to western collectors, nor did they rely to any extent on charms or magic. I made several field trips with Maulana, one of the best hunters and best flute players. His flute was a sort of badge of office and got us into a few areas where strangers weren't especially welcome. Also, he enjoyed a jam session when the day's work was done. Once when a big snake

102

escaped under a rock ledge, I suggested he play his flute and lure it out. I got a very disdainful look as an answer. Jogis are particularly skillful at tracking reptiles to burrows or other hiding places and digging them out. Much of the time, however, they wander about investigating likely habitats and keeping their eyes open just like herpetologists anywhere. Madge was once driving down a canal road with two Jogis when a large dhaman glided across ahead of the jeep. The Jogis were out and after it in an instant, but the snake took refuge in a large thorny bush. They tried to poke it out, then they borrowed a match and set fire to the bush. The snake burst out and dived into the canal. After the reptile escaped, the Jogis shrugged and climbed back into the jeep leaving the bush burning briskly. The Jogi's real secret weapons in collecting are time and endurance. Investment of enough man-hours will always produce specimens, and a hunting party may spend days in the field living under conditions most westerners would find unendurable.

Jogis handle venomous snakes in a casual and insouciant manner, but one that shows considerable ability to judge snakes' temperament and probable reactions. Nevertheless, they are bitten occasionally. They claim no immunity to snake venom but do rely upon various secret remedies. Although they often sought our help in other illnesses, when Laung, the headman of the tribe, was bitten by a cobra and lay almost completely paralyzed, they were not interested in our offer to treat him. During the fourteen months we were quite closely associated with them, the tribe lost one man to a cobra bite and had two other serious snakebites. On the other hand, they had several bites that were trivial.

Although Jerry Anderson and I were good friends, his herpetological collections were destined for the Royal Scottish Museum, and Mustapha Koncieczny was a collector for Robert Mertens of the Senckenberg Museum in Germany. The presence of three professional herpetological collectors in Karachi was a godsend for the Jogis, and they played us against each other shamelessly. Luckily Madge and I did not begin buying from them until we had been in Pakistan long enough to have some idea of the abundance and distribution patterns of many reptile species. The Jogis quickly learned that we were not interested in buying a reptile specimen without locality data, so they invented localities apparently on the principle that the farther away from Karachi a snake was taken, the more rupees it would bring. This led to some obviously silly reports such as a lowland snake allegedly taken at a Himalayan hill station in midwinter, but sometimes it was difficult to be sure.

It was impossible to deal with the Jogis without becoming unspeakably annoyed with them, yet they were such flamboyant charlatans and such barefaced rogues that anger evaporated quickly. Their hospitality seemed free and spontaneous, although they spoke not a word of our language and we very little of theirs. They had no difficulty in accepting us— were we not all snake hunters? As I finished my last class with my students at the Postgraduate Medical Centre, Maulana, in the full regalia of a Jogi of Sind, strode into the laboratory with all the arrogance of a brigand chief. He gave me a great bearhug and handshake and stalked out. "Well," I said to my Sindhi technician, "This will never happen to me in Indiana."

Returning to Indiana was not easy for any of us. Although we were back in our same house and I was in the same department of the medical school, Madge and I had a different view of ourselves and of the world. We had been sahib and memsahib in a new and terribly poor nation carved from old British India, and we had experienced the anomalies and paradoxes that resulted from this. Moreover, there had been changes in values and attitudes in the United States. A president was assassinated a few months after our return, and there was talk of war in a region we knew as Indo-China. Sometimes we felt indeed like strangers in a strange land. It was even more difficult for our girls. Brooks was in her senior year of high school, and the other girls in the grades. All found an environment quite different from the one they'd left in 1958 and the one they'd been living in for more than four years. And on top of everything else, it had been four years since we'd experienced a Midwestern winter.

In Pakistan, April and Holly were able to ride horses. After returning to Indianapolis Sherman and Madge bought them a horse of their own.

CHAPTER 6
MEXICO

For those who began a career in herpetology in the United States about the middle of this century, Mexico acted like a powerful magnet. It has one of the richest amphibian and reptile faunas in the world, and, in 1946, it was relatively little known. There was a long border with the United States, a friendly population, and a steadily improving highway system. Universities and museums with programs in herpetology sent small expeditions south of the border every year, and a certain number of enthusiastic individuals simply went down on their own. If they spent a month or so in a good area, there was an excellent chance they'd return with a species or two new to science, some significant field observations, and lots of good stories.

Mexico's amazing biodiversity comes from many factors. For openers, Mexico extends from the Temperate Zone well into the tropics. Along its volcanic spine are permanently snow-capped peaks that provide a subarctic environment. In the northern part of the country are two major deserts, while large areas of tropical rain forest once covered the southern and eastern lowlands. There are many miles of seacoast, and large, upland, freshwater lakes. Additionally there are some isolated areas with distinctive topography and vegetation. Over some two million years, Mexico has been on a highway between North and South America and has received migrants from both directions, but it has also had unique biological areas where species have evolved and persisted. Although advanced civilizations existed in Mexico before arrival of Europeans, their impact on the environment was not marked except in a few areas such as the valley of Mexico and parts of Yucatán. However, this has changed during the last two centuries with the expansion of agriculture, destruction of forests, and, more recently, industrial and urban pollution. Mexicans aren't particularly kind to their environment nor concerned about it, and their reasons are not hard to understand. They want more comfortable lives for themselves and their children, and if this means diverting streams, lowering the water table, clearing the hillsides, and eliminating a certain number of unique plant and animal species, it seems a cheap enough price to pay. In all fairness, however, there have been improvements, and a growing environmental conscience has been evident in the last few years.

My first herpetological collecting trip to Mexico was with Phil Smith and Max Hensley, following a route Phil had taken before. We crossed the border at Brownsville, Texas, and drove south along the old Pan-American Highway. For more than 200 miles the highway goes through flat, dull country made up of cultivated fields and semidesert. Then, over some fifty miles, the terrain becomes hilly and the vegetation dense and luxuriant. Adobe houses tend to be replaced by thatch. Hillsides are cultivated, no matter how steep, but there are still areas of tropical thorn forest. Some kinds of trees are always in flower and epiphytic orchids and bromeliads cling to their branches. Scavenging caracaras and flocks of green parrots appear, and long, baglike nests of oropendolas hang from branches. During late summer, thousands of butterflies drift across the roads, and you occasionally glimpse the iridescent blue wings of a morpho. About thirty miles southwest of Ciudad Mante is Cascada El Mico, in 1963 an almost undisturbed jungle waterfall on an incredibly blue stream. Today it's utilized for hydroelectric power and much of its beauty gone. About 130 miles down the old Pan-American Highway from Ciudad Mante is Tamazunchale, "Thomas-n-Charlie" to generations of gringo biologists who know it as the gateway to the real tropics. Wild monkeys apparently were found here until about 1950, and it is a favorite spot for orchid collectors. Along this section of road I had my first experience with some classic tropical American reptiles—the green iguana, the boa constrictor, and the dangerous big pit viper the local people call cuatro narices (four nostrils). However, my only unpleasant encounter was with a medium-sized, mottled brown treefrog I picked off the pavement on a rainy night. A few minutes later I rubbed my eyes and immediately felt intense burning pain and tears so profuse that I could no longer drive the car. It was easy to identify this amphibian as the ranita lechosa *(Phrynohyas venulosa)* a species well known for its irritating milky skin secretion.

Phil, Max, and I followed the highway southwest of Tamazunchale and began a long, winding ascent onto the Mexican plateau. Here we stopped for the night in the old Spanish colonial town of Querétaro. This is the city where Maxmilian, the French-backed Austrian ruler of Mexico, was executed by rebels under Benito Juarez in 1867, and where the current Mexican constitution was signed in 1917. Its outstanding architectural feature is a great aqueduct completed in 1738 to bring water from the hills to the city. It is still in use. In 1960 the city was best known as a center of opal mining. At the time of our visit, vendors hawked jars of rough, poor quality opal on every street corner. We didn't buy any but photographed some of the old churches, caught a turtle and some toads and lizards on the edge of the city, and headed north to San Luis Potosí. Here we turned east, descended from the plateau, and rejoined the Pan-American Highway at Ciudad Mante. It was on this leg of the trip we made our most unusual herpetological find. Digging into the decayed base of a yucca, we uncovered a stocky, wormlike reptile about eight inches long. We first thought it was one of the blind snakes that are not especially uncommon in this section of Mexico, but its head was the wrong shape and its tail too long. Although we could hardly believe it, we'd caught *Anelytropsis,* a unique burrowing limbless lizard restricted to eastern Mexico and known at that time from fewer than a dozen specimens. Its nearest relatives live in Southeast Asia and are equally rare.

The 550-mile highway loop with Querétaro near its southwestern edge was destined to become familiar to Madge and me. And largely because of Brooks who has always been the linguist of the family. In Big Bend in 1955 she picked up

Spanish phrases from her schoolmates. A few years later in Pakistan she soon became reasonably fluent in Urdu, so much so that she made up handy phrase books for her mother to use in the bazaars and for me to use in taking medical histories from patients. Going to school with children of a dozen or so nationalities, she learned a few words from all of them. When we returned to Indiana she finished her last year of high school at Broad Ripple in Indianapolis. Her Spanish teacher, also a longtime friend and neighbor, arranged for her to spend the following summer in Guanajuato, Mexico. This is another old Spanish colonial city of the plateau and one with a decidedly macabre distinction. Whenever the tombs of the great cemetery become overcrowded, mummified bodies of those who have not paid their rent are disinterred and put on display in a large hall.

In college, Brooks majored in Spanish and made other trips to Mexico as well as to Spain and Italy as part of her study program. When she graduated in 1967 she accepted a teaching position at a bilingual school in Querétaro. The Mexican culture and environment suited her, and a year or so later she met Miguel Cervantes. His parents, both artists, lived in San Miguel de Allende in Guanajuato state. Miguel taught in the language department of the University of Querétaro. He and Brooks opened an English language school in Querétaro and were married in 1971. Today, Miguel is an executive of the Kellogg Cereal Company plant in Querétaro, which has grown tenfold into a major industrial city. He, Brooks, and their daughter, Natasha, live quite comfortably in a renovated seventeenth century house in the old part of the city. The result of all this is that Madge and I make trips to Mexico with some regularity.

Herpetological collecting was a major activity until the late 1980s. A scientific collecting permit wasn't much harder to get than an Indiana fishing license. Later, for various reasons, regulations on collecting in Mexico became very strict and the cost of a permit very high. Today (1996) it is virtually impossible to do legal herpetological collecting in Mexico without support of a major university, zoo, or museum. However, with reasonable luck, it is still possible to observe and photograph some of the region's interesting reptile and amphibian fauna.

Mexico

Most of our trips to Mexico have been by car. On our first trips, we followed the old Pan-American Highway as Phil, Max, and I had, and this is still my favorite route. However, the route south of Laredo on the new Pan-American Highway is quicker, and we can drive from the border to Querétaro in a day if we push ourselves; however, the terrain is less interesting. A couple of times we have crossed farther west at Eagle Pass and once far to the west at Nogales.

Our 1989 trip was particularly memorable. We reached Laredo a few days before Christmas with a cold wind blowing and temperature close to freezing. Evidently every Mexican in Texas was going south to spend Christmas, for there was a long line at the customs house. However, it moved quickly because it was too miserably cold to check cars for contraband. About fifty miles south of the border, we were told by the police that the highway was impassible because of ice. So we headed down the Rio Grande valley and picked up our old route near the southern tip of Texas. We reached Victoria, Tamaulipas, after dark and in a sleet storm. Next morning the fountains and palms on the motel grounds were coated with ice. We wore heavy jackets to breakfast in the unheated restaurant where the coffee and eggs were cold as soon as they reached the table. After driving about a hundred miles to the south, we turned west toward the sierra, which was blanketed with clouds. At about 2000 feet, the entire tropical thorn forest was white with hoarfrost. Each leaf, flower, tendril, and spiderweb had a coating of tiny ice spicules. After a climb of another 2000 feet or so, we emerged onto a desert landscape with bright sun and vultures and coyotes scavenging the carcass of a donkey. Next day we reached Querétaro about twenty-four hours behind schedule. When we retraced the route about a month later, we couldn't see much change in the thorn forest, but the citrus orchards had suffered and piles of oranges were rotting by the roadside.

For anyone interested in Mexican natural history, there is an interesting trip from Querétaro to the lowland a bit northwest of Tamazunchale. When Madge and I first drove the route in 1968 there were no gas stations, but gasoline could be purchased on a sort of ad hoc basis in villages. As we left the

Mexico City highway our landmark was Pico Bernal, an imposing pyramid of rock that is visible for miles. Here the overgrazed and heavily farmed landscape of the plateau gives way to the Sierra Madre Oriental, and the road becomes a long series of hairpin turns, first climbing and then descending into the valley of the Rio Extoras which flows intermittently through an island of Chihuahuan desert where ocotillo, catclaw, and leather plant are characteristic flora. It's the only place I've ever found peyote, the orange-sized cactus whose flesh, when eaten, produces vivid hallucinations. I once tried a small slice. It was very bitter and had absolutely no effect on me. Some interesting reptiles are found here, but I've never had any luck collecting them. However, I've done better with scorpions, getting one or two that were unusual records. East of this valley, the road climbs steeply to the village of Pinal de Amoles at about 8600 feet. Drooping pines and oaks originally made a thick, humid forest here, but much of it has been destroyed. In the patches of forest are salamanders of several species, the largest and most spectacular being black with a row of red or gold chevrons the length of its body. Most of the mountain reptiles are small. The bright blue males of one of the spiny lizards (*Sceloporus*) are quite conspicuous. A more secretive but plentiful lizard is a bronzy skink with sky-blue tail. East of Pinal is an equally steep descent into the valley of the Rio Jalpan. This is a rocky area of dense thorn forest interspersed with cultivation and with cypress along the river. Collecting in the thorn scrub isn't easy but there are interesting snakes and lizards. This is the only place I've found the tropical rattlesnake—a road kill. Also on the road we collected a tricolor kingsnake that would become one of the specimens Hugh Quinn used to describe a new subspecies. A little black and yellow striped snake that I picked up bit me at the base of a finger and caused sharp pain like the sting of a wasp followed by swelling of my finger. This was one of numerous "venomous nonvenomous" snakes that would be subjects of future research. On one collecting trip I met a party hunting tigrillos (probably ocelots) in the scrub. They weren't particularly friendly.

The road east of the town of Jalpan goes through rolling

country into an area of red soil with sparse forest of oak, madrone, pine, and sweet gum. The underlying rock is limestone with caves and sinkholes. In the caves live salamanders, and the limestone crevices are home for some curious lizards and small snakes. This area also has enormous numbers of phalangids (daddy longlegs) and millipedes. Here Madge and I met a field party from Texas A&M University collecting herpetological specimens for our friend, Dr. Jim Dixon. We spent several hours turning logs and swapping information.

As you continue eastward, the route continues to be hilly. The vegetation becomes decidedly tropical with many bromeliads and orchids. Birds include the green jay, kiskadee flycatcher, groove-billed ani, and great black hawk. In this area on a winter trip, we saw where spiders had spun dense webs between the phone wires for a distance of two kilometers or so and trapped an immense number of insects. Spiders aren't supposed to be social creatures but at least this one species is. Incidentally, visitors to many parts of rural Mexico are often puzzled by hairy looking gray objects the size of a baseball or a little larger attached to telephone wires and other objects. Sometimes there are tiny flowers sticking out of the mass. This is a bromeliad related to Spanish moss.

On this lowland route about 1987 we noticed plastic, boxlike objects attached to trees. These were traps for the Africanized or "killer" bees that have been steadily moving northward from Brazil since 1957 and have now crossed the U.S. border. On our trip to Chiapas in 1988 Madge was attacked by a swarm, but got into the car after being stung only twice. Her hat and clothing protected her, but there were bees in the car when she picked me up about a mile up the road from where she was attacked. The Africanized bees are a strain of the common honeybee and their venom is no more toxic; however, they are much more aggressive and attack in greater numbers. There have been quite a few deaths from multiple stings.

Enrique and Sonia Cervantes, Miguel's parents, had an avocado ranch on a hillside near Tacámbaro in the state of Michoacán. This is not far from where a volcano suddenly erupted in a cornfield in 1943. The mountain forest is mostly pine, oak, and madrone. In a valley near the house is an attractive waterfall where I watched water onzels and hummingbirds. Having grown up in the Midwest where there is only one species of hummingbird, I've become intrigued with the numerous species found in the southwestern U.S. and Mexico, although I can seldom identify them. Because most of our trips to Tacámbaro were in winter, we did not see many reptiles. The ranch house was the site of occasional parties where pulque and mescal flowed freely. These beverages have a lower alcohol content than tequila though the ultimate effect is similar. All come from the fermented sap of giant agaves or century plants. Each bottle of mescal traditionally contains a worm that is eaten by the person who finishes the bottle. In the commercial product, the worm is plastic.

In 1968 and 1969 we went farther west to the Pacific coast of Mexico. Our destination was Manzanillo, then a sleepy little seaport that hadn't yet became a port of call for cruise ships. We stayed at an old hotel on the beach and divided time between swimming, loafing, and hunting reptiles. Perhaps the most interesting specimen we collected was a small escorpion or Mexican beaded lizard, one of the world's two venomous lizards. It's closely related to the Gila monster but is not a desert animal; instead it prefers the lowland dry forest. Over the years, I've heard of three or four bites by captive beaded lizards. In all cases, intense pain was the chief problem. One individual showed signs of shock, but all recovered with no permanent damage. Another interesting reptile we found near Manzanillo was the Mexican python or chatilla. It's a dark brown snake about three or four feet long. It's not truly a python, nor is it a boa, but it seems to be a primitive snake with no close relatives. It is a secretive burrower, but the one we got was on the road at night. Another nocturnal reptile we got was a gecko related to the leopard geckos we knew so well from Pakistan.

On one of our night road-running trips, the headlights of our jeep failed totally. We fell in behind a truck and relied on its headlights until we came to the steep, narrow road that led to our beachside hotel. At this point, Madge drove and I lay on the hood of the jeep and used a flashlight to pick out the edges of the road. The trouble apparently was a minor flaw in the electrical system that a local mechanic quickly fixed next day.

Car trouble has plagued us on several Mexican trips. In 1968 we burned out a clutch in a thinly populated section of northern Mexico. Very luckily we got a tow to the "taller mecánico" in the tiny village of San Roberto Junction. By another bit of luck, Madge, April, and Holly got a ride to Querétaro with friendly tourists. I stayed with the car until it was repaired next day. This gave me a chance to do some collecting in the surrounding desert. I found, among other things, a horned lizard and a Mojave rattlesnake. Vinegaroons were unusually plentiful. This large arthropod looks somewhat like a scorpion and is called "madre de alacranes" by many Mexicans. However its "tail" is a long filament rather than a series of segments. It doesn't have a sting, but at the base of the tail are glands that expel an aerosol of acetic and caprylic acids with a strong vinegar smell, hence the name. Vinegaroons are fierce predators; I found one in the act of eating a small snake. Vinegaroons do well in captivity feeding on crickets and other insects.

Genuine scorpions are common throughout Mexico. There are many species, only a few dangerous. Prior to about 1960 there were hundreds of deaths from scorpion stings annually, mostly among infants and small children in the western states of Jalisco, Guerrero, Guanajuato, and Michoacán. Thanks to better methods of treatment and more rural health centers, deaths are uncommon today. Large centipedes also are common. One we caught near Ciudad Valles was about nine inches long and nearly an inch wide. Centipede bites are quite painful but almost never serious.

The tarantulas common in the southwestern U.S. and Mexico are impressive looking but very inoffensive. They almost never bite, but some have irritating hairs on their abdomen. Several species such as the Mexican red-knee tarantula have become popular pets. For several years, Brooks had a big yellow and black tarantula named Faust, although it probably was a female. Tarantulas usually hide in burrows or under various sorts of cover, but occasionally many of them may be seen wandering in the open for reasons unknown to me. Black widow spiders are very plentiful in Querétaro and some other upland Mexican states. In some stone fences there seems to be one in every crevice. In spite of this, spider bites don't appear to be very common.

In 1966 we flew from Costa Rica to Oaxaca where we joined Charles Bogert and his wife, Mickey, of the American Museum of Natural History. They regularly spent summers in that region. We spent a week dividing our time between collecting amphibians and reptiles in the cloud forest, visiting archeological sites, and shopping for handicrafts in roadside markets. Like so much of Mexico, Oaxaca suffers from deforestation and overcultivation. However, in the patches of upland forest at 7000 to 9000 feet, we found trees adorned with bromeliads, orchids, and mistletoe. Many wildflowers bordered the trails. Tiny salamanders of the genus *Thorius* were plentiful, and we got an alligator lizard with lichenlike greenish markings and several kinds of small snakes. We saw a few turkeylike chachalacas, a bird I'd seen before only in the valley of the lower Rio Grande.

We've made other trips into southern Mexico by car, more or less following the Gulf Coast. In late February, jacaranda, copa de oro, poinciana, bombax, and other trees are in bloom. In the wetlands are many birds such as the tiger heron, sungrebe, jacana, ringed kingfisher, and mangrove swallow. Basilisks basking on branches are the index reptile. In addition to the boa constrictor, there are four other large snakes in the Gulf lowland. Largest is the cribo or culebra arroyera that reaches a length of about ten feet and is closely related to the indigo snake of Florida. It is usually found near water and eats almost any vertebrate it can swallow, but is an especially voracious snake predator that has been reported to eat boa constrictors more than five feet long as well as large pit vipers. The voladora is a slender, black and yellow arboreal snake that occasionally reaches a length of about nine feet. Its name, "flyer," refers to its agility both in trees and on the ground. In Tabasco I saw one of these snakes about seven feet long stretched on the branches of a tree sticking out of the water near the bank of a pond. Judging the water to be no more than a foot or two deep, I jumped from the bank in an attempt to grab the snake. I landed in water above my waist and ruined the camera around my neck. The snake made a clean getaway. Another snake in the seven to eight foot range is the Neotropical whipsnake or chirrionera. Near Tlacotalpan in Veracruz, Madge and I found two eighty-inch whipsnakes full of eggs killed on the road in almost the same spot but a few hours apart in time. An hour or so later we caught a third smaller snake that apparently had just laid a clutch of eggs. A very dangerous big snake is the pit viper, identical with the terciopelo of Costa Rica and called cuatro narices in northern Mexico. I've never found one of these snakes more than about thirty inches long, but Phil Smith and Max Hensley encountered a huge one in Veracruz when road cruising at night. They decided it was too big a snake to fit any of their containers and let it crawl off the road. All these big snakes are fairly common even in heavily populated agricultural land. They eat a wide variety of food including rodents and small chickens, and find shelter in mammal burrows, drains, and rubbish heaps.

In 1988 we visited the great Mayan ruins at Palenque which had been abandoned by their builders and hidden by jungle when the Spaniards arrived in the seventeenth century. There is still good tropical forest in this area. Friends of ours from Querétaro when driving at night saw a tigre (jaguar) on the road. We were not so lucky, but we did see such birds as toucans, white hawks, motmots, and noisy flocks of parrots and caiques. Reptiles were uncommon, but we watched the courtship of two large rock iguanas. Our next trip to southern Mexico was during a period of civil unrest in Chiapas. We had no real trouble but weren't able to move around very freely. However, in November 1996 we drove north in the Yucatán Peninsula to Campeche and Uxmal and had no trouble at all. There were practically no cars with U.S. plates on the roads, but the Mayan archeological sites at Uxmal, Kabah, and Edzna had busloads of mostly European tourists. Yucatán is a region of low limestone ridges covered with dense, low forest. At the large Xtacumbilxunan Cave we saw a great flock of Vaux's swifts with their nests around the cave entrance. Gaudy orange orioles, big blue and black jays, and flocks of little green parakeets were common enough on back roads around Uxmal, but wildlife generally wasn't conspicuous. This was especially true of reptiles. Except for a few rock iguanas and a snake that slipped away before we could identify it, there were none to be seen.

When I was in college, Mexican food was the campus tamale vendor with his pushcart. Today, some sixty years later, there's a plethora of Mexican restaurants in the Midwest, but the selection of foods is still limited. Some are dishes popular throughout much of Mexico, but many are characteristic of the northern states bordering the U.S. Tourists often are surprised to find not all Mexican dishes are spicy. Although fiery jalapeño peppers are popular almost everywhere, some regional dishes of the plateau and western Mexico are quite bland but tasty. Jicama is one of the Latin American vegetables that has recently reached the markets of Indianapolis. However, the fruit (tuna) and young pads (nopales) of the big prickly pear that are staples in many parts of Mexico don't seem to be well-known north of San Antonio. There are several good tropical fruits such as cherimoya, mahmey, and grenada china that are seldom seen north of the border.

For those with adventuresome tastes, there is cuitlacoche (corn fungus), armadillo, agouti, and ant pupae. In lowland Veracruz, a well-known hotel was, and perhaps still is, noted for monkey. Iguanas, both the common green species and the garrobos or rock iguanas, are eaten, particularly in western Mexico. Around lakes of the plateau, axolotls may be seen in streetside markets. Sea turtle eggs were formerly harvested in immense numbers because, in addition to tasting good, they are believed to enhance virility. The turtle nesting grounds are now protected, but I'd guess there is still a black market for eggs. Some freshwater turtles including the unique and uncommon tortuga blanca (*Dermatemys*) also are prized for food. Until the last half-century or so, most of these wild animals were eaten by relatively small local populations, but today rapid transportation and refrigeration have made them available to a wide market, often with disastrous results for the animals.

I have not heard of snakes being eaten in Mexico, but rattlesnakes are used in folk medicine. In the northern part of the state of San Luis Potosí, the Pan-American Highway traverses a desolate bit of desert. As long as we have traveled this route, the local Indians have been engaged in selling wildlife to tourists. On our early trips, they sold mostly small mammals such as ground squirrels and weasels, and birds such as hawks and parrots. However, about 1987 they began to display many dried snake carcasses on crude frames. In 1987 we estimated there may have been two hundred carcasses; in 1990, 1991, and 1994 there were fewer, and in 1996 the carcasses were smaller. Most of the snakes were clearly rattlesnakes, but some were nonvenomous snakes with rattles sewed to their tails. Those who buy the carcasses evidently use them as soup stock or grind them to powder, which is then made into pills. Brooks learned that polvo de cascabel or rattlesnake powder is an old and valued folk medicine in rural Querétaro and is used in treating cancer and for skin and kidney diseases. AIDS patients desperately seeking unconventional remedies make up a new group who try it. A survey of Hispanic patients in a Texas border hospital indicated about a third had used rattlesnake remedies. In addition to having no known therapeutic value, snake tissues may contain dangerous salmonella bacteria. Salmonella infections don't often kill previously healthy persons but frequently are lethal in cancer and AIDS patients.

For many of us who enjoy foreign travel, one of its main attractions is the chance to try new and unusual foods. The downside of this is that sometimes what you eat makes you sick. The gastrointestinal disorders that afflict travelers have a long list of colorful names and an even longer list of remedies and preventatives. When we were living in Karachi, the major topic of conversation at the cocktail parties given by the British and Americans was the state of one's bowels, closely followed by the behavior of one's servants, the weather, and one's chances of getting out of this hellhole. At the Basic Medical Sciences Institute, our microbiology department did several studies on causes of diarrheal disease both in foreigners and in the local people. With the relatively primitive techniques available to us in 1958, we rarely found a microbial cause when the patients were infants or young children or adults with mild illness. When patients were adults with more serious illness, we could more often find a cause, usually bacteria of the shigella or salmonella type, the dangerous amoeba (*Entamaeba his-*

tolytica), or the pesky protozoan, *Giardia*. Today, with extensive studies in many parts of the world and more sophisticated diagnostic techniques, a lot more is known. It now appears that much of the diarrhea that takes such a high toll among infants and small children and causes travelers such discomfort is caused by toxin-producing types of the common colon bacillus (*Escherichia coli*) that is in virtually everyone's gut. Viruses of several kinds are another common cause, but it takes a specialized laboratory to identify them. Old favorites like shigella are still around and important. The advent of AIDS has brought to the forefront several bacteria and protozoa that we previously ignored or didn't know existed. In the immunologically impaired they produce devastating illness, but they can attack healthy persons also. Even with the best available techniques, some 20 to 30 percent of diarrheal disease can't be ascribed to any particular microbe.

Among U.S. tourists, Mexico is notorious for "Montezuma's revenge" or "the touristas" but this is largely a function of the large number of tourists who go there. European tourists have just as much trouble in some of the Mediterranean countries and the East Indies. High-risk areas aren't necessarily tropical. Intestinal parasites are common in the former USSR. When Madge visited the Ukraine in 1990, water free of parasites and dangerous radioactive nucleotides had to be obtained from vending machines rather than public drinking fountains. And I recall a Pakistani student getting travelers' diarrhea in Indianapolis.

A lot has been written about precautions to take when travelling in Third World nations. Many follow a simple rule with beverages—don't drink anything that doesn't come out of a bottle. However they sometimes forget the ice in their drink must come from safe water. Even straight gin won't kill all parasites. A common rule with foods is "cook it, peel it, or forget it." But it's easy to become careless and take chances. Also, if you're trying to win the hearts and minds of people or dickering with snake charmers for rare reptiles, remember that offering food and drink is one of the oldest gestures of hospitality. Refusal can be seen as impolite and unfriendly. "My country will never know what my stomach's suffered on its behalf," is a plaint I've heard at more than one Third World dinner party.

The speaker would doubtless have a favorite medicine to take after such meals and probably a second medicine to take if the first didn't work. Enterovioform was popular when we lived in Karachi, but it has some serious side effects and is rarely used today. If someone is going on a short vacation trip to some romantic and probably expensive tropical resort, a trip that would be spoiled by forty-eight hours or so of stomach cramps and diarrhea—I recommend taking Pepto-Bismol tablets with each meal. There are some antibiotics that work just as well but are more expensive. Protection is not 100 percent by any means. Bacteria and viruses are fiendishly clever in developing resistance to drugs, so it's a good idea to carry some tablets of Imodium or Lomotil. These drugs don't cure anything, but they usually relieve symptoms until your immune system takes over. If you have bloody diarrhea, fever, or illness that lasts a week or more, you need medical care and probably microbiologic studies. Anyone with severe diarrhea, particularly a small child, needs to replace water and salt that is lost. This can be done with ingredients in any kitchen, but it's more convenient to carry packets of the UNICEF or WHO formula that can be dissolved in water. On our longer trips in Pakistan, Mexico, and elsewhere, we carry something for quick relief plus an antimicrobial with as broad a spectrum as possible. Bactrim is our choice at the moment.

Chapter 7
Scuba Diving

In 1966 Madge and I attended a symposium on venomous animals and their venoms held at the Instituto Butantan in São Paulo, Brazil. Established in 1899 by Dr. Vital Brazil, it was one of the first institutions to produce antiserums for snakebite, and it remains an important center for research on venomous animals. It is also one of São Paulo's major tourist attractions where crowds of people watch hundreds of dangerous snakes sunning on grassy lawns in front of their little hemispherical houses.

The symposium was attended by many internationally famous scientists, among them Prof. Robert Mertens of Senckenberg Museum in Frankfurt am Main, Germany. He and I weren't on particularly good terms. To begin with, he didn't like Americans because they had bombed his city and museum. More specifically, I'd worked in Pakistan, which he considered his territory and I had beaten him in publishing a major work on the herpetology of that nation. However, he took a liking to Madge and conceded that I had some qualifications as a herpetologist. Two years later he named a skinny, bad-tempered racer snake from the Baluchistan desert for the two of us. In 1975 Prof. Mertens died from snakebite. Like Karl Schmidt, he didn't think the snake that had bitten him was a particularly dangerous species. Also like Schmidt, he kept a record of his symptoms that concluded, "für einen Herpetologen einzig angemessene Ende" (for a herpetologist, a singularly appropriate end.)

At the time of our visit, it was the custom of the Instituto Butantan to send plantations and rural health centers vials of

The participants at the Simpósio Internacional sôbre Venenos Animais held at the Instituto Butantan in 1966. From left to right: (back row) unknown, Konrad Klemmer, Mahmood Latifi, Alphonse R. Hoge, Janis A. Roze, L.D. Brongersma, unknown, Joseph R. Bailey, Madge R. Minton, P.E. Vanzolini, Sherman A. Minton, (front row) Ilya S. Darevsky, Bertha Lutz, Robert Mertens, and Marcos A. Freiberg.

antivenin in exchange for live snakes—which arrived at a rate of about fifty boxes a week. For us symposium delegates, the unpacking of the boxes was like a quiz show as we guessed at the identity of each new snake. Mertens and Ilya Darevsky, Russia's leading herpetologist, made the best scores. The snakes that were sent in greatest numbers were the Brazilian rattlesnake, the jararaca, and the false jararaca which looks much like a North American hognose snake.

When we left São Paulo, our destination was the San Blas Islands off the coast of Panama. Madge had seen some beautiful molas (cutwork and applique fabric panels) done there. We left Panama City in a four-seat plane and shortly landed on El Porvenir Island, which is just above sea level. At that time, it supported a few thatch huts and a small tourist court that we had to ourselves for our first day. Later we were joined by a Frenchman

Scuba Diving

and an American lady. When I greeted her in Spanish, she said plaintively, "Doesn't anyone here speak English?"

There were just two things to do on El Porvenir aside from lying in a hammock—visiting the Indian village and skin diving on the reef. We did all three but the diving was by far the best. This was our first underwater view of a coral reef, and we were utterly enchanted by the colorful and oddly shaped fish and the variety of corals, sea urchins, plume worms, sponges, starfish, and shells. After our second day on the reef, I said to Madge, "After this, who needs LSD?"

One of the Indians had a dugout and, for a small fee, took us to the mainland for herpetological collecting. On a night trip in the cutover forest we caught several frogs including a couple of medium-sized treefrogs that looked in no way unusual. Next day I took one out to photograph and saw the bright green body, yellow legs, and incredible red eyes of *Agalychnis callidryas*. This Central American treefrog is now familiar in photos and graphics to most of the world's people and is virtually the logo of the Neotropical rain forest. But in 1966 comparatively few people knew it existed, and I never thought I'd be lucky enough to see one. On a day trip, we stumbled onto ruins of an old U.S. Army airbase where Madge saw, pressed into a concrete step, the name of a man who had flown echelon with her in 1944. We caught a basilisk in a nearby building.

The next leg of this trip took us to Costa Rica where we took the train from San José to La Fortuna in the Gulf lowlands. Here we were guests of the Taylor family, descendants of President Zachary Taylor, who had moved to Costa Rica after the Civil War and now owned a large banana and cacao plantation. We had good herpetological collecting. Especially memorable were the many little strawberry frogs hopping about in bright daylight and protected by a toxin in their skin secretions. After dark we caught a small, bright pink snake with a black head and yellow collar. This was a young mussurana that would be black as night when full-grown at a length of about six feet. It is a snake-eater that feeds largely on venomous pit vipers.

After our trip to the San Blas Islands, Madge and I decided we should learn scuba diving. We took a course taught in

Indianapolis by the British Sub-Aqua Club. It involved rather rigorous instruction both in the swimming pool and in the classroom. However, Indiana is not a great place for scuba diving. The most available sites are flooded rock quarries where the most exciting thing you're likely to see is an automobile someone drove into the quarry for any of a variety of reasons. Aquatic life is bluegills, crawfish, and the occasional turtle, although once we found dozens of tiny jellyfish with bells about the diameter of a nickel.

Our first saltwater dive was made at Islamorada in the Florida Keys. I've had a longtime relationship with southern Florida. About 1927 my father thought seriously of moving to Florida, and we lived several months at Miami Beach. The ocean was virtually in our front yard and I learned to swim in a strip of calm water between a sandbar and the beach. I also learned that those pretty blue balloons that occasionally floated in on the tide could give a fierce sting. During our stay in Florida I contracted a series of infections, one of which was probably creeping eruption. This is an invasion of the skin by larvae of dog or cat hookworms and is acquired by contact with fecally contaminated soil. Because humans are an unnatural host for the larvae, they crawl about aimlessly and produce intense itching. Although it eventually clears up, it can go on for weeks. My illnesses and a hurricane evidently caused my parents to decide against a move to Florida.

During the Christmas holidays of 1949–1950, Madge, Brooks, my brother, John, and I drove down the west coast of Florida. At Tampa we were guests of the Hillsborough County Herpetological Society, probably one of the first amateur herpetological clubs in the country. Mr. and Mrs. W.W. Logan entertained us in their home, and club members told us where and how to hunt for reptiles in southern Florida. They recommended we stay at the little village of Estero slightly south of Fort Myers. This was our base for collecting at the edge of the Everglades. Here I saw my first wild alligator, otter, and bald eagle. Nearly all the amphibians and reptiles were species new to me. I was surprised at how big the gopher tortoise is; I'd thought it would be about the size of a box turtle. The following year, Madge, Brooks, and I went back to Estero. The motel where we stayed was in a citrus grove and guests were free to eat all the fruit they wanted. We went to Marco Island, then an empty strip of beach, where we dug up handfuls of little coquina clams, and dipped crabs from an inlet. With these and a few supplies from the grocery, we ate well for very little. On both trips we caught handsome blue-black indigo snakes.

On our diving trip in 1970 we found southern Florida much more heavily settled and more expensive, although reptiles were still plentiful in places. We were somewhat disappointed with the diving. Corals were sparse and the fish less colorful than we'd expected. The wreck of a Spanish galleon was just a few timbers sticking out of the sand.

Our next ocean diving was at Grand Cayman the following summer with the British Sub-Aqua Club. Grand Cayman had not yet become a center for tourism and international banking, and things were pretty relaxed and easy. A major attraction for Cayman divers is the wall. This is actually the edge of a tectonic plate that plunges almost vertically downward some 5000 feet. It is an uncanny sensation to swim out over the edge of the wall and look downward an endless distance into darkness. I had the good luck to spend about fifteen minutes of my sixty-fifth birthday on the wall at depths of ninety to one hundred feet. Another nice feature of Grand Cayman diving is that many good sites can be reached by swimming from shore without depending on a launch.

The undersea life was beyond our wildest expectations. On our first few dives there was so much to see we developed a sort of sensory overload; later things began to fall into place and we could identify and understand what we were seeing. Most of the life that forms the underwater "landscape" is animal rather than plant. Branching corals that may be broad and flat or round and pointed, and sea fans, sea whips, and other gorgonians make up the shrubs and bushes. Sponges assume fantastic shapes and often are brightly colored. Some cauldron sponges are big enough for a diver to crouch inside them. Great hemispheres of brain coral have colorful feather duster worms sprouting from their crevices.

Through this landscape move a fantastic assortment of fish. Parrot fish are almost sure to catch your eye, for they are bright-colored, moderately big, and rather deliberate; they have strong, horny jaws and graze on coral. The softer part of the coral is digested, while the crushed mineral part is expelled almost continuously as the fish swim about. At least some parrot fish sleep on the bottom in clear bubbles they secrete around themselves. On our second dive, Madge and I looked up to see a five-foot barracuda circling us. These great, trim, silvery fish have a look of menace about them and, based on stories I'd heard, a bad reputation. I pulled my dive knife out of its sheath wondering if it would do the least good if the fish attacked. This was probably as stupid a thing as I could have done, for the glint of metal is one of the few things that will, in rare cases, cause a Barracuda to attack a human. However, our barracuda gave us a brief inspection and disappeared like magic.

Angelfish are easy to recognize. They are of medium size, strongly compressed laterally, and have large, often metallic looking scales. Butterfly fish are similar but smaller and often have vivid patterns; some have long, tubular snouts. On a dive in rather shallow water, we saw three small black and white fish with very long, fluttering dorsal and caudal fins that gave them the shape of a reversed letter C. They were in a tiny coral grotto and in intense, frenetic, hovering movement. We later identified them as young jackknife fish. As they mature, their fins shorten and they have a less bizarre appearance.

Earlier this century, the Cayman Islands were site of a great green turtle fishery. Today this has become a turtle farming operation that causes some controversy among environmentalists, since eggs from wild turtles are necessary to keep it going. Be that as it may, it isn't unusual to see sea turtles of various sizes when diving around the islands.

Needless to say, we were interested in the land reptiles as well. All the species are small except for an endemic iguana that is now very scarce. Virtually every Caribbean island has its distinctive *Anolis* lizard species; big islands like Cuba and Puerto Rico have many. On our 1971, 1972, and 1978 visits to Grand Cayman, we saw only the single native anole, easily recognized by its blue dewlap. However, on our 1984 visit we saw a second species, particularly in the outskirts of Georgetown. We collected a few specimens and found it to be the Cuban brown anole, an aggressive colonizer that has now established itself over nearly all of Florida where it has supplanted the native green anole in urban areas. It's gained a foothold in Mexico, South America, and on several Caribbean islands. What will happen on Grand Cayman is anyone's guess.

We collected a couple specimens of a slender, racerlike snake about a yard long. Snakes of this genus (*Alsophis*) occur on many Caribbean islands and in mainland South America. By conventional criteria, they are typical harmless snakes. However, in 1873 Felipe Poey, a Cuban physician and naturalist, reported a case of envenoming by the snake he knew as jubo which is almost identical with the snakes we caught on Grand Cayman. Because the snake had been tormented, Poey thought its anger had caused it to secrete venom, an idea borrowed directly from writings of Moise Charas in 1670. However, Poey was the first naturalist to report a venomous bite by a presumably nonvenomous snake. Today there are several reports of venomous bites by *Alsophis* snakes.

A man we met on Grand Cayman told us he had snakes in his well, and just before we left the island he brought us two. They were members of a Neotropical genus (*Tretanorhinus*) unrelated to water snakes of the United States. In 1984 we got a third type of Cayman snake—a wormlike blind snake about six inches long.

We made scuba diving trips to other islands in the American tropics. All had rich undersea life that was similar in many ways to that at Grand Cayman, but on every trip and almost on every dive we saw something new. At San Salvador in the Bahamas, the popular attraction was a bottlenose dolphin that enjoyed playing with divers. At several dive sites the bottom was white sand, which means excellent visibility and different fish. This is good habitat for stingrays; we saw several species, some having a spread of four feet or so. Rays don't use their sting unless pinned down or otherwise restrained, so divers aren't at risk unless very unlucky or foolish. Stepping on a ray in shallow water is how most people are stung. I saw my first sting when an intern at San Diego Naval Hospital. I had no idea what to do. Thinking the sting might be in the wound (it almost never is), I infiltrated the whole area with local anaesthetic so I could probe for the sting. This relieved the sailor's pain and he had no other alarming symptoms. Not all victims are so lucky. In addition to being venomous, the sting of a big ray can do a lot of mechanical damage. Stings to the chest or abdomen can be fatal.

A spectacular fish we never saw anywhere but San Salvador was the flying gurnard. It is about a foot long and has huge, vividly marked pectoral fins that it spreads when alarmed. This was also the only place we saw venus's-girdles. They are iridescent, undulating, ribbonlike creatures about fifteen inches long. They belong to the group of comb jellies, odd animals with no close relatives.

South Caicos was the only area where we saw sharks on several of our dives. None were more than about five feet long and none showed any sign of hostility. We got accustomed to barracudas, although we never saw another as big as the one we had seen on our second dive at Grand Cayman. South Caicos had many large conch which were good eating. There, we first saw an odd invertebrate we called "tigertail." It could be as much as four feet long, about the thickness of a broomstick, transversely banded yellowish and dark brown. It was years before we identified this creature correctly as a very elongate sea cucumber.

An interesting activity we saw on many dives was the cleaning of larger fish by smaller fish and invertebrates such as shrimp. Most of the cleaner fish are small elongate species of gobies or wrasse, but young of larger species such as angelfish and hogfish may act as cleaners. Larger fish go to particular stations to be cleaned, and cleaners identify themselves by colors and gestures. Cleaners pick parasites from the skin and also from the inside of the mouth. A similar activity can be seen on land where several species of birds pick ticks, leeches, and other parasites from cattle, rhinoceroses, turtles, and crocodiles.

Since I was often the only physician in the group, I occasionally had to care for peoples' ailments. Luckily those in our dive club were healthy and the trips short, so I had no serious problems. External ear canal infection (swimmer's ear) was common and painful. It's easier to prevent—dry your ear canals carefully—than to cure. I carried hydrocortisone and antibiotic drops

Scuba Diving

that were usually effective. The commonest injuries by marine life were fire coral stings and wounds by sea urchin spines. I found hydrocortisone spray quickly relieved the pain of fire coral stings. Sea urchin spines were troublesome. Immediately after the injury, which is painful, a dark purple discoloration may appear around the puncture. This is from a harmless fluid in the spines but is disconcerting. The spines are fragile and very hard to extract. After my first few attempts, I found it best to leave the spine fragments to the body's defenses or to the skill of a qualified surgeon. On at least two islands, I was told by local folk that urine—especially urine of a virgin—would dissolve the spines. Virgins were in short supply in our group, so I did not try this remedy. The only severe marine animal injury in our dive group occurred on a trip that I didn't take. One of our friends surfaced at night under a jellyfish and was badly stung on her neck and shoulders. In addition to intense pain, she developed faintness and difficulty breathing. She was given oxygen in the dive launch and recovered in a relatively short time. She and her husband brought me a jellyfish they said was identical to the one that inflicted the sting. I identified it as the Caribbean sea wasp (probably *Carybdea marsupialis*), a species known to be dangerous.

Contrary to television commercials and travel brochures, not all Caribbean islands are lush and green. Of those we visited, none were. Aside from patches of pantropical trees such as coconut palms and poinciana and some fringing mangroves, most of the vegetation was semiarid scrub with cacti often dominant. Introduced animals such as goats, pigs, dogs, and cats have been very destructive to native fauna and flora. The mongoose, introduced on some islands to control rats and snakes, has been especially hard on birds and reptiles. The larger reptiles such as iguanas and boas are now extinct or threatened on islands where it occurs.

Tiny geckos of the genus *Sphaerodactylus* are characteristic of the Caribbean islands and usually live under rubbish or in crevices. Somewhat larger geckos often live in buildings. Some are restricted to the Caribbean region, others are widespread in the tropics. On Middleton Cay near South Caicos, Madge caught a small spotted snake with an orange tail. It was one of the so-called dwarf boas (*Tropidophis*). These most-ly West Indian snakes are thought to be intermediate between the primitive boas and pythons and the more advanced snakes. The orange tail tip is probably a lure. Resembling an insect larva, it may be used to attract the small lizards that the snake eats. Such lures are used by several other kinds of snakes including young copperheads.

Our dive trip in January 1978 was to San Salvador, where we'd played with the dolphins and scooted around the wreckage of a small freighter sunk in 1902. We came back to bitter cold and high winds. On January 25th, I heard something about a blizzard warning on the car radio but didn't think the guy was serious. However, a few hours later the temperature had dropped below zero, snow was blowing almost horizontally, and you could hardly see ten feet ahead. For the first time, I really understood what a "white-out" can be. It's an eerie sensation.

Next morning there was five feet of snow across our drive-way right up to the garage door. Juniper bushes that were higher than our heads were just sticking out of the snow. When you're in a ridiculous situation, you do ridiculous things. Madge and I raised the garage door and dug a tunnel about fif-teen feet long. Then we snuggled up in it like a couple of marmots until things got too cold. Later we cut blocks of snow and built a snowhouse. This is something we'd done several times before when the girls were young, but the 1978 snow-house was our best effort. Our cat couldn't figure what was going on and didn't find the snowhouse very comfortable.

Next day we dug out the driveway enough to get our four-wheel drive Subaru out to the street, and life more or less returned to normal. The snowhouse didn't collapse until March 13th. On March 19th there were still patches of unmelted snow in the woods south of Indianapolis, but many salaman-ders were active. Large piles of dirty snow were still in city parking lots on April first.

They say tropical storms never hit Bonaire and the diving is always good, but when Madge and I arrived there in November 1984, water and debris swirled through the ground floor of our seaside hotel and rain poured down as a storm moved away from the island. Bonaire lies off the northwestern

Scuba Diving

coast of Venezuela and is one of the Netherlands Antilles. Like many West Indian islands it is rocky and quite dry. There are the inevitable coastal mangroves and palms, but the most conspicuous plants in most places are large cacti. There is not much agriculture, but goats are everywhere.

The day after we arrived, seas were too rough for diving so I set off inland along one of the narrow but well-paved roads. As I left the hotel grounds, I saw a nice adult of the endemic anole clinging to a wall, but by far the most conspicuous lizard was a big fellow, some fifteen to eighteen inches long, heavily built, and predominantly brown in color. Part of its tail was a bright blue-green and there was an intensely brilliant patch of this color on the dorsal surface of each hind foot. Not all the lizards seemed to have this patch and it may have been a breeding color. When I returned to Indianapolis I found these lizards are a species restricted to Bonaire, but closely related to the little racerunners I'd known as a boy from the knobs near New Albany. They were everywhere on the island except in the mangroves and on the beaches. The big ones were fond of basking on the many stone fences. We caught one that had fallen into the cistern of an abandoned house and saw the skeletons of others that apparently had perished in such places. They are, at least to some extent, scavengers. We saw them eating crabs that had been killed on the roads, as well as feeding on the remains of their own kind. They don't seem to have many enemies. They probably are a little too small for human food in normal times, but feral cats and small boys with slingshots must account for some.

Twice in thick underbrush we saw large green lizards that I'm pretty sure were the common iguana. This species probably does end up in the cooking pot and this may explain its apparent rarity.

We didn't see any of the cosmopolitan, house-dwelling geckos that often share your hotel room in the tropics, but there were many small geckos under rocks and in trash piles. During my first couple days of searching, I thought there were a half-dozen species, but soon it was clear that there were just two with marked pattern and color differences between the sexes and between adults and juveniles. We found a few larger geckos with plump tails that I recognized as the turnip-tail gecko, a species widely distributed in the Caribbean region. With the geckos in rubbish piles were bright yellow scorpions that apparently weren't very dangerous, and big black and red triatomid bugs of the type that suck blood and carry Chagas' disease.

Eventually the weather cleared and we had some good diving off Bonaire. We saw many of the common Caribbean reef fish as well as some that were new for us. Among the most grotesque were frogfish that look like lumps of sponge or coral, crawl along the bottom, and attract prey with lures that stick up from their snouts like automobile antennas. Boxfish with bodies encased in a bony carapace and fins that project and vibrate like little propellers were common. Moray eels were commoner here than at other Caribbean reefs where we had dived. Large jacks and groupers also were plentiful.

Shortly before we left, we rented a car and drove to the north end of the island to see the flamingos that are common in the coastal lagoons. Going inland on an unimproved road, we came to a little pond surrounded by fairly dense tropical forest. There were many small birds including yellow-headed parrots, hummingbirds, orioles, and warblers newly arrived from the U.S. Under a rock we found a small lizard amazingly similar to the mole skink of Florida. It was not a skink but was a microteiid, probably *Gymnophthalmus lineatus,* the only live specimen of this lizard group I've ever seen.

That night the air began to fill with mosquitoes emerging from larvae that had been developing in the rainpools left by the storm. Next day we left Bonaire. This was our last scuba diving trip.

In December 1984 Madge and I returned to Karachi for the twenty-fifth anniversary of the Jinnah Postgraduate Medical Centre that I had helped establish. There had been many changes since 1962. The city was much larger. There was much more automobile traffic and fewer animal-drawn vehicles. However, house crows and kites were still plentiful in the downtown area. We were guests of Hassan and Aysha Javeri whom we had known from the years that we lived in Pakistan. Their house in Hill Park had been at the extreme eastern edge of Karachi then; now it was well inside the city. At Hill Park I saw green bee-eaters nesting in a sandy bluff and sunbirds feeding on flowers. Many other city birds such as hoopoes, bulbuls, wagtails, and bushchats were numerous. Garden lizards (*Calotes versicolor*) and several smaller lizard species were still to be found. The Russians had built a large steel mill complex not far from the Malir Cantonment, and there was much light industry. We made three auto trips to Tatta, Haleji Lake, and a small waterfall in the Sind Desert where we had camped several times in years past. Land in the lower Indus valley was extensively cultivated with sugarcane and rice. Kingfishers, merlins, and other birds were numerous, and we saw a mongoose and several snakes along irrigation ditches. At Haleji Lake, 1962 signs warning visitors of crocodiles had been replaced by signs saying the lake was a crocodile refuge. There were thousands of coot, also many paddy birds, egrets, cormorants, drongos, and green parrots. Purple moorhens, anhingas, dabchicks, and fishing eagles were at least as plentiful as they had been twenty-five years previously. A group of British bird watchers appeared to be having a marvelous time watching the avian variety and the show of a Tatta Jogi with his cobra and sand boa.

Javeris took us on an outing to the seacoast at Cape Monze. With snorkeling gear, we saw a variety of fish quite different from those in the Caribbean. Sergeant majors were similar but larger, there was a blue and white angelfish, a small wrasse or blenny with bright orange and blue bars, and other fish we couldn't identify. We also saw a medium-sized octopus and some small jellyfish.

We spent Christmas with Dr. M. Sharif Khan at Rabwah in the Punjab. Dr. Khan is Pakistan's leading herpetologist. He took us into the field, but it was too cold for most reptiles. The lowland along the Chenab River is cultivated, but surrounding hills are bare and rocky. Mynas and crows were the only common birds, but we also saw green parrots, Indian rollers, rufous-backed shrikes, and a small owl. The Ahmadi Moslems of Rabwah have a strict dress code for women, and Mrs. Khan had some suitable clothes made so Madge could appear in public. Rabwah has a small but vociferous Christian population that sang and beat drums incessantly during the night before Christmas.

In early December 1984, Dr. Minton informed me that he and Madge were visiting Pakistan to attend the twenty-fifth anniversary of the Jinnah Postgraduate Medical Center, Karachi. After the celebration, they planned to visit Rabwah to see my herpetological laboratory, and study local herpetofauna.

The Mintons were to stay with me for three days, December 23rd–26th, 1984. They reached Faisalabad (forty-eight miles south from Rabwah) by plane, and I was to pick them up from the airport. Unfortunately, there was a misunderstanding on my part about the arrival time of their plane. When I reached the airport, the Mintons had already left for Rabwah by hiring a taxi. When I returned home, I was relieved to find my guests comfortably enjoying tea and local sweets with Rashida (my wife). Rashida had called one of my former students to act as an interpreter, since she could not understand American English. Thank God, both guests were in high spirits. When I apologized for the misunderstanding, Dr. Minton said promptly, "Oh no, anyway we passed each other on the way. Had we met at the airport, we could not have recognized each other." The laughter which followed took away all of my embarrassment. Yes, he was right, I had in my mind their picture on the title page of their book, *Venomous Reptiles* (1969) — now they were so different!

Later Rashida told me when she opened the door for the guests, Dr. Minton, keeping his eyes low (respecting Muslim tradition about women) asked me "Is this Dr. Khan's bungalow?" I said, "Yes, yes, please, come in." It was the first time in our thirty-five years of married life that I heard her speak English.

I took the Mintons to several places around Rabwah in search of local herpetofauna, but nothing was sighted — it was cold, 4–15°C. The hills surrounding Rabwah attract the attention of visitors, and for Dr. Minton they were exceptionally attractive, since he had been collecting geckos, agamas and snakes on similar rocks in Balochistan. He wished to climb a hill, but we ended up turning around due to his aching back. I vividly recall him taking out a couple of Tylenol capsules from a yellow wrapper and swallowing them. I told him about my knee pain and he promptly gave me two Tylenol capsules, which I kept for long time in my laboratory as a souvenir of his visit. We had climbed the hill enough to look out over the town. The view was quite scenic. Beyond the city near the horizon, a meandering silvery trail of the Chenab River was visible, with an intervening belt of deep green wheat crops. The symmetrically arranged streets and roads of the town looked nice. Dr. Minton took several photographs. Due to the cold temperatures, however, no animals were to be seen.

On the last day of the Minton's stay, we visited a nearby artificial jungle, Chak Bahadur Plantation, 3 miles north. We went deep into the jungle looking for animals. Only a few *Mabuya* slipped from one thorny bush to the next.

Muhammad Sharif Khan

CHAPTER 8
ALPHA HELIX

 In 1972 Dr. Bill Dunson, a herpetologist especially interested in physiology of marine reptiles, was organizing an expedition to study sea snakes. This is a family of about fifty species, all venomous. They are found in the tropical and subtropical Pacific and Indian Oceans nearly always in relatively shallow water over the continental shelves. Taxonomically they are a difficult group, and in 1972 little was known of their biology. Dr. Dunson contacted me because I had some knowledge of these snakes and their venoms from my years in Pakistan, I was a qualified diver, and I could serve as physician for the expedition. So in early December of 1972, I was once again on my way to the South Pacific.

After brief stops at Honolulu, Midway, and Kwajalein, I joined the research vessel *Alpha Helix* at Ponape in the Caroline Islands on December 7th—thirty-one years after the raid on Pearl Harbor. On that day, Ponape had belonged to Japan.

The *Alpha Helix* was a sturdy little ship 133 feet long with a beam of thirty-one feet. She was diesel powered and fitted with thoroughly modern biology laboratory facilities. Accommodations were cramped but comfortable and the food was excellent. Her captain and crew were former Navy and Coast Guard personnel. The scientific party in addition to Dunson and me included Hal Cogger (Australian Museum, Sydney), Hal Heatwole (University of New England, Australia), Emerson Hibbard (Pennsylvania State University), John McCosker (Steinhart Aquarium, San Francisco), Harold Puffer (University of Southern California),

The *Alpha Helix*

Roger Seymour (Monash University, Australia), and Nobuo Tamiya (Tohoku University, Japan).

For an island in the far Pacific, Ponape is fairly large and heavily covered with vegetation. It is of volcanic origin with high, steep cliffs. We spent three days there. By far our most interesting trip was to Nan Madol where great temples and other structures have been built from huge prisms of basalt that look like the Lincoln Logs I played with as a child, but on a gargantuan scale. I felt amazement and tremendous respect for the effort and skill of the early Polynesians who had built these structures. I have much the same feeling when I see Mayan and Aztec pyramids, all built with only human muscle to move the stone and never a wheel to help.

We got no sea snakes at Ponape but large green skinks and some smaller lizards were common. Along the shore were terns, gulls, frigate birds, and reef herons. Wildlife was scarce in the forest; I saw a parrot and a few other birds completely unfamiliar to me.

It was a curious sensation to be back at sea on a small ship after almost thirty years; feeling the motion of the deck under my feet, hearing more or less familiar sounds, sleeping in a

Alpha Helix

The crew of the *Alpha Helix:* (front row) Harold Heatwole, Harold G. Cogger, Nobuo Tamiya, Sherman A. Minton; (middle row) Walter Garey, Roger Seymour, Harold Puffer, Gerald Robinson, John McCosker; (back row) Max Webster, Emerson Hibbard, and William Dunson.

narrow bunk. Many times during the Pacific war, I wondered if, when this madness was over, I would meet someone who had been on the other side. Now one of my shipmates was Nobuo Tamiya, who had been a pilot in the Imperial Japanese Navy. He didn't talk much about his war experience, but I got the impression he'd had a tougher time than I. After the war, he'd resumed his education in biochemistry and became outstanding in this field. He was the first to isolate and crystallize a toxin from sea snake venom.

While we were underway, some member of the scientific party kept a bow watch during daylight. For six days of calm seas, there was little to see except flying fish, a few birds, and one whale. Then we sighted the coast of New Guinea and saw another whale, a large hammerhead shark, and large violet jellyfish with orange tentacles. On the beach were thatched huts and dugout canoes. We began trawling in MacCluer Gulf about sunset and continued until midnight. The trawls brought up many sea creatures I'd never seen including little sea dragons, strange flat fish, several types of crabs, and lots of crinoids.

Crinoids belong to the same phylum as starfish, but with jointed branches that end in a flowerlike calyx, they look more like plants. I'd known crinoids as fossils from my boyhood at New Albany where we called the little stony cylinders and discs "Indian beads." Shortly before midnight we caught our first sea snake, a slender snake of the genus *Hydrophis* which includes nearly half the sea snake species.

During the next forty-eight hours we caught about thirty-five more sea snakes. Our first attempts were something like nineteenth century whaling. When a snake was sighted from the *Alpha Helix,* we put a Zodiac boat in the water with one person operating the engine and someone with a net in the bow. He would try to dip up the snake. This was exciting but not very effective, for the snakes had every advantage in maneuvering and diving. A far better technique was to collect at night with the ship anchored and lights rigged over the side. As the snakes surfaced, they were dipnetted from the ship or from a Zodiac. We found that a snake spotted within a few minutes after it surfaced could nearly always be caught. I thought it like a submarine that's been kept down until her batteries and air supply are exhausted. The longer the snake stayed on the surface, the more likely it would escape by diving. Eventually our physiologists found the snakes weren't staying on the surface primarily to ventilate. They could replace the air in their lungs in a few seconds. What they were doing was thermoregulating—warming up at the surface after having been down a half-hour or so in deep, cool water. The snake we caught in the greatest numbers was Hardwicke's sea snake (*Lapemis curtus hardwickii*), a stocky species about a yard long and more inclined to bite than most sea snakes. We also caught three species of *Hydrophis*.

Late on December 19th, we arrived in the Indonesian port of Ambon. The next afternoon I climbed into a jeep taxi with seven local people and the driver and rode to the hills behind the city. It was hot and dry. The houses were constructed mostly of palm thatch. Characteristic trees were sago palm, durian, clove, and nutmeg. Rusting antiaircraft guns and tanks left from the Japanese occupation were in fields. I got reacquainted with flying dragons, skinny little lizards whose ribs and skin form a pair of winglike structures that they use to glide from one tree to another. The largest lizard on the island is the water dragon, which is about a yard long and has a sail-like fin on its back. Others in our party caught several of them, and one of the lizards bit the collector's finger powerfully enough to drive its teeth through his nail and give me my first patient with injury from a reptile bite. They also caught a small reticulated python badly infested with ticks, and a cuscus, an opossum-like arboreal mammal. Local people came out to the ship in canoes with seashells, crabs, monkeys, parrots, lizards, hawksbill turtles, and a single tree snake.

Shortly after leaving Ambon, we made a deepwater trawl about midnight. This brought up bright red shrimp, arrow worms, a luminous salp, and some small but grotesque fish with huge jaws and light organs still feebly glowing.

We spent Christmas in Darwin, Australia, celebrating with a ship's party at the Fannie Bay Hotel. Darwin has amazingly high tides. We stepped off the ship from the main deck—when we returned, we stepped onto the pilothouse. This is disconcerting even if you're sober. The next day, David Lindner and John Wamby, two of Hal Cogger's herpetologist friends, took Hal, Bill Dunson, and me on a field trip. In the afternoon I had my first look at Australia's distinctive wildlife. In the scrubby forest we saw two wallabies and a magnificent frilled lizard. At the edge of a large marsh were hundreds of magpie geese and masked plovers along with smaller numbers of white spoonbills, ibis, and storks. After dark we returned to the marsh to hunt water pythons. The first one we saw was about five feet long and was crossing the road. About a half-hour later, Lindner staggered out of the marsh looking like one of the Laocoon Group with an eight-foot python wound around him. We caught three more pythons and a few other snakes. A rain shower brought out many frogs including the big waxy green treefrog, *Litoria caerulea.*

From Darwin we headed due west toward Ashmore Reef. This is part of a reef complex between Australia and the Indonesian

12 January, 1973 aboard RV *Alpha Helix* anchored off Ashmore Reef, Timor Sea.

"Rose at 06:30 to the most perfect day of the trip to date — light cloud, no wind and the sea a glassy lake. After breakfast we all jumped into the boats and crossed to the exposed reef edge where we looked for fish and snakes. Finding some Emydocephalus, Aipysurus fuscus *and* A. foliosquama *I spent some time with Sherm and Red Hal [Heatwole] photographing the reef and the snakes. Later, we joined the others in a snake filming session. After lunch on board, we worked our way over to the reef sand flats and eventually to East Island. The water was so clear that we easily observed, and in most cases identified, snakes on the bottom in 10-15 metres of water. Snakes were so abundant that we made no effort to catch all that we saw: one* Acalyptophis *and many* Aipysurus laevis, A. fuscus, A. duboisii, A. foliosquama *and* Emydocephalus annulatus."*

"(Ŝit's bloody difficult not to resort to anthropomorphism in interpreting snake behaviour when you work with Aipysurus laevis; *today, as on several previous occasions, a large specimen was investigating crevices on the bottom when it looked up, spied me hanging in the water above it, grinned (I swear!) and headed straight for me and wound itself around my fins. I KNOW it was just curious and wouldn't bite me but there was something in that grin that made me chicken out and so I caught it before I had a chance to test my conviction."*

"Returned to the ship at 17:15 and, apart from time out watching 'Suddenly Last Summer' in the Library, worked until retiring at 00:30."

The above diary extracts are from the only field trip I ever shared with Sherm Minton, and records a day in his company. Apart from this expedition, I got to know Sherm and Madge from correspondence (especially our annual exchange of Christmas cards) and from irregular and usually brief personal encounters during their time spent in Australia and at occasional conferences. My first and lasting impression of Sherm was of a gentle, dedicated polymath who found something new to excite him every day. Yet there was the occasional hint — especially a lowering of the brows — that he did not suffer fools gladly.

Certainly when we were together he displayed great depth of knowledge, tolerance, humour and this immense enthusiasm, which we shared, for the natural world and the revelation of evolution. Yet I can hardly claim to have known the complete *man*.

But like others I've known who gave so generously of their knowledge, wisdom, and company, I will always value the time I spent with Sherm and deeply regret his passing.

Hal Cogger

island of Timor. For unknown reasons, this area has an amazing concentration of sea snake species and individuals. In two weeks we collected 367 snakes of eleven species and saw many more. More importantly we made observations on many species that had never before been seen by biologists in their natural habitat. Here scuba diving equipment and underwater cameras proved most helpful, although the gear we had was nothing like that available today. I have unforgettable memories of those reefs, none sharper than that of a five-foot Stoke's sea snake cruising along in a manner that could only be described as majestic, with a group of about six small black and gold pilot fish clustered about its head. This was the largest snake in the area reaching a length of about six feet and almost as heavy-bodied as a boa constrictor although not nearly as muscular.

The commonest species was one of a group of sea snakes with tiny heads, long slim necks, and heavy bodies. They were once in the appropriately named genus *Microcephalophis,* which is no longer recognized. This body form allows the snake to search with its head and neck in small crevices and burrows while the body provides stability in the water. The Ashmore small-head is a deep diver that we sighted once at 145 feet; undoubtedly it goes deeper. It also has extremely lethal venom. We'd not have known this had it not been so plentiful, for the yield of venom per snake is minute. However, Tamiya and Puffer collected enough venom to determine it was about twice as toxic as venom of the Australian tiger snake, then considered the most deadly land snake. The Australian press had been following the *Alpha Helix* expedition with some interest; it must have been a slow news summer and this made a good story. However, there was a problem: we didn't know the identity of the snake. It seemed fairly close to *Hydrophis belcheri,* a very poorly known snake described in 1849 from a specimen collected near New Guinea and named for the captain of the ship that brought the first specimen to the British Museum. So we called it Belcher's sea snake, and under that name it made the *Guinness Book of Records* as the world's most venomous snake. Later it appeared in Michael Crichton's novel, *Sphere,* which is a somewhat sensationalized story of underwater exploration. After Hal Cogger and I had studied preserved specimens with some care, we

146

Hydrophis coggeri, the snake with the most toxic venom of any known species

decided it wasn't *Hydrophis belcheri* but might be *H. melanocephalus* known from the South China Sea and Ryukyu Islands. Considerably later, after collecting more specimens in the Coral Sea, I decided it was an undescribed species and had a paper in press calling it *Hydrophis pericorallion,* but before it appeared, a Russian marine biologist who had reached the same conclusion gave it the name *Hydrophis coggeri.* This was a great disappointment, for I did hope my name would be linked to a sea snake of some sort.

Another common sea snake was the turtlehead or egg-eating sea snake (*Emydocephalus*), a rather small species that feeds entirely on fish spawn. Its fangs and other teeth are very small. We were never able to extract venom from this snake—it may be harmless. We evidently arrived at the mating season for these snakes and saw them often as pairs. Their courtship was like that of many land snakes and took place on the bottom at depths less than fifty feet with the male rubbing his chin on the head and neck of the female. If she was feeling friendly, the male would press his whole body against her, twist his tail around hers, and insert one of his two penises. Copulation could last at least a half-hour. If the pair were disturbed, the female would swim off, more or less dragging the male along.

Hal Heatwole and I did most of the diving and decided two of the Ashmore species were deepwater snakes rarely seen where depths were less than fifty feet, two were mostly confined to water less than thirty feet deep, three preferred thirty-five to seventy-five-foot depths, and three seemed to show no preference. The pelagic sea snake, as its name implies, was seen only at the surface but often in deep water.

For diving and snorkeling, we wore wet suits even though they were sometimes uncomfortably warm. This was partly for protection against snakes but even more so to protect from one of the most dangerous of marine creatures, the sea wasp or box-jelly (*Chironex fleckeri*). This is a jellyfish whose bell—instead of being discoid or hemispherical—is roughly cube-shaped and up to ten inches wide. Its unusually heavy tentacles may extend seven feet and contain millions of stinging cells. Although it wasn't scientifically described until 1956, I believe I'd heard of it during the war. There were stories of survivors from ships and planes who were floating in the water and who died quickly and in great pain from the sting or bite of an unknown creature. A snake was usually suspected, but sea snake bites are totally different. They are almost painless and the venom acts slowly. There have been about fifty proven fatalities from box-jelly stings in Australia. An antivenin is now available, but persons badly stung may die before it can be given. In our dive boats we carried a large jar of alcohol to treat stings on any exposed skin. Luckily we never used it, for it's now known this is bad treatment. Vinegar or other mild acid is best. I never encountered a box-jelly while diving but saw several from the ship.

Ashmore and the nearby Scott and Hibernia Reefs were an almost undisturbed marine environment at the time of our visit. Malay and Indonesian fishermen gathering sea cucumbers went there occasionally—in fact it was those fishermen who'd made the first sea snake collections. There were indeed lots of sea cucumbers, most of them looking like huge caterpillars. When disturbed, they evert much of their internal viscera as a mass of sticky threads. Small, elongate carapid fish live as quasiparasites in the gut of sea cucumbers, swimming in and out through the anus. Giant clams with royal blue mantles were a common sight on the reefs. During the war, it was believed that these would close like a mousetrap on a hand or foot; this is not true. One of our underwater demolition teams lassoed a giant clam and hauled it onto the deck of the *Brooks*. I was asked if it was good to eat. Being ignorant but cautious, I said no. However, on the *Alpha Helix,* Tamiya said quite the reverse and we ate chunks of the muscle raw. It was excellent.

Coral growth was spectacular in places, particularly discoid, lacy, pale blue or greenish yellow corals several feet in diameter and huge brain corals. Sea anemones were common and often harbored two or three brightly colored clown fish among their tentacles. A bright blue starfish was very common, and we saw a few of the venomous crown-of-thorns starfish.

Of the larger sea animals, we saw sharks regularly but not real often. Their only reaction to us seemed to be a mild curiosity. After a dive during which I'd photographed a fairly big nurse shark, Hal Heatwole said to me, "You ought to have seen the shark that was watching you." To get a rough idea of shark predation on snakes, we baited hooks with dead sea snakes and on one occasion caught a large tiger shark. One of our party who was removing the jaws of this shark cut his finger on a tooth and quickly developed an ugly infection. We had no bacteriologic culture media, but we did have microscopes and stains, so I made a smear from the infection and saw what seemed to be streptococci. Luckily we had an antibiotic that promptly took care of things.

Schools of as many as forty dolphins were a common and pretty sight. We saw sea turtles occasionally. The hawksbill seemed the most common species. We watched one feeding on the bottom in about thirty feet of water and saw evidence of turtle nesting on sandbars.

The reefs were barely above water but some had bushes growing on them. Surprisingly, we found a few rats and geckos around an automated lighthouse. Even odder were the moths and dragonflies that occasionally came to the ship's lights as we lay anchored. They must have flown or been borne by winds for many miles.

From Ashmore Reef we sailed eastward between Australia and New Guinea, stopping at several islands. Except for a small crocodile, we saw little that was extraordinary. On January 23rd, I left the *Alpha Helix* at Cairns, Australia. Here I met Madge who had flown to Brisbane, rented a car, and driven up the coast to Cairns. This was not considered a safe trip during the wet season, but she made it and collected several interesting reptiles en route including a frilled lizard and a bearded dragon. We spent the next week in the region near Cairns. On one trip we walked up Tully Gorge through a maze of huge boulders overhung by tropical forest. The stream was clear with deep pools. Birds were plentiful but nearly all unfamiliar. At one spot were many nests of a small swift, made with gelatinous dried saliva mixed with lichen and other debris. Nests like this are the source of genuine Chinese birdnest soup. Along the stream we saw water dragons and many smaller lizards, and large butterflies and dragonflies. Going inland from Cairns one can climb onto the Atherton Tableland and enter a mixture of grassland, tropical rainforest, and dry, open eucalyptus woods. There are many large termite mounds. Particularly on night trips, we saw wallabies and bandicoots, which are marsupials that look like very large rats. We also saw smaller ratlike mammals under cover in forest. There were many kinds of birds, most of which we could only identify to types such as rails, pigeons, hawks, and finches. We collected a variety of lizards —nearly all skinks.

Around towns and cultivated areas, the commonest vertebrate animal often was the cane toad. This huge toad is native to the American tropics but was introduced into the cane-growing parts of northern Australia in 1935 to control pest beetles. It failed in this and, lacking predators and parasites, became very plentiful. Because of its large venom glands, it is lethal to such Australian predators as snakes, monitor lizards, kookaburra kingfishers, and the marsupial cat as well as to domestic cats and dogs. For native Australian frogs, it may be both a predator and competitor.

We spent two days on Green Island off Cairns. This was a wooded island with many birds. The deep cooing of pigeons made afternoons pleasant. There seemed to be two species, one large and white, the other smaller and bronze with green markings. Frigate birds, curlews, and reef herons were numerous. Reptiles were limited to small skinks and geckos. Coral around the island showed damage by crown-of-thorns starfish, but sponges, sea urchins, and anemones seemed to be thriving. Fish were of the same types seen at the reefs of the Timor Sea.

On January 31st, we flew from Cairns to Sydney where we rented a car and drove northward to Hal Heatwole's university at Armidale, which is in mountainous country between Sydney and Brisbane. On the drive up, we stopped at a rocky mountain stream where we saw a redbellied black snake. It flattened its neck somewhat like a cobra and slipped into the water. Somewhat farther along the route, a large, stocky lizard ambled across the road. This was our introduction to the blue-tongue skink. It stuck out its wide, cobalt blue tongue in a startling threat display. However, these are placid, gentle lizards. They thrive in captivity; one that we gave to the Bechtels is alive as this is written twenty-two years later. Local people said these lizards keep tiger snakes out of your yard, but a few days later we overturned an old billboard and found a blue-tongue skink and tiger snake curled within a few inches of each other.

We had three pleasant days in Armidale with Hal Heatwole and his family, much of the time spent in the mountains surrounding the city. The landscape reminded us of parts of the southern Appalachians. Herpetological collecting was good, particularly since almost everything we caught was a species new to us. Australia is a continent of lizards and most of them are skinks. In most parts of the world, skinks are small, elongate, smooth-looking lizards with short legs and long tails. However, in Australia skinks may be large, stocky, rough-scaled, or short-tailed and may live in desert, park, or rain forest where they run, swim, climb, and burrow.

We left Armidale early in February and drove toward Sydney. As we left the mountains, the temperature rose to 110°F in the shade. When we got to a motel in Newcastle, Madge asked the proprietress for some ice. She relayed the request to one of her children who asked, "Ice? What's the lady want ice for?" Newcastle is one of the last places I saw steam locomotives in use on a regular scale.

Meanwhile, the bearded dragon Madge had caught several weeks previously laid seventeen eggs, which we carefully kept from excessive heat and drying. She hoped a customs official would ask what they were so she could say, "dragon eggs," but this didn't happen. Regulations on taking reptiles out of Australia were fairly liberal in 1973, and Hal Cogger helped us get permits. We paid for excess baggage but got some interesting creatures back to Indiana. Most were given to zoos and museums.

CHAPTER 9

THE SOUTH PACIFIC AND AUSTRALIA

In August 1975 I was again following paths from World War II as I left Manila on the *Alpha Helix*. This expedition had broader goals than the one to the Timor Sea. Dunson, Heatwole, Roger Seymour, Tamiya, and I were chiefly concerned with sea snakes, while Willard Hartman and Robert Trench (Yale University), James and Karen Porter (University of Michigan), Michel Pichon (James Cook University, Australia), and Renato Garcia (Philippine National Museum) were involved with coral reef ecology. Both the Porters were very experienced divers, and Pichon had formerly been with the Cousteau group. The captain and most of the crew of the *Alpha Helix* were the same as those who had been on the Timor Sea expedition. Our first stop was the naval base at Subic Bay where we visited a jungle survival school and spent a night in the rain forest under "survival" conditions. It wasn't bad, but I prefer shipboard living. In the jungle, I saw hornbills, some spectacular butterflies, and a large caterpillar I feared we might be required to eat. I've eaten a few kinds of insects but draw the line at caterpillars. Hal Heatwole told me he'd tried wichety grubs and said they tasted like shrimp stuffed with sawdust. After dark there was much bioluminescence in the ground litter but from no obvious source.

From one of the local people I got a paradise tree snake, one of the so-called flying snakes that flatten their bodies and glide from tree to ground or tree to tree. I brought this little reptile back to my lab in Indiana and kept it about a year, but it never performed for me. However, some species of this genus (*Chrysopela*) definitely do glide. A friend of mine had a large golden tree snake that got loose in his house. We found it on the uppermost shelf of a closet from which it promptly launched itself into the air.

From Subic Bay we cruised to the long, narrow island of Palawan. The reef at Green Island had a rich variety of colorful soft corals, starfish, and tunicates or sea squirts. These are animals of another group intermediate between invertebrates and vertebrates, although in their adult stage they look like little jars or vases. Swimming among them were butterfly fish, moorish idols, parrotfish, and a batfish, all species new to me.

We found no sea snakes but had two unusual snake hunts along the Barbicon River where mangrove snakes were plentiful in trees bordering the river. These snakes were about four feet long, slender, and jet black with bright yellow crossbands. They rarely moved and catching them was like picking fruit. The mangrove snake is mildly venomous. All of us who caught the snakes were bitten, but none of us showed any signs of envenomation—probably because we didn't give the snakes a chance to engage their fangs which are in the rear of the a upper jaw. Tamiya and I obtained venom from several mangrove snakes and found it was almost like syrup. In a 1-percent solution, it killed mice in small doses. Its action seemed to be on the blood and blood vessels rather than on nerves.

In the trees along the river we saw a small troop of monkeys, white parakeets, a large yellow woodpecker, and a large kingfisher. Among the mangrove roots we saw archerfish— noted for knocking down small insects with droplets of water ejected from their snout.

We did not see sea snakes until we entered the Visayan Sea, which is in the center of the Philippine Archipelago. Here they were plentiful with sea kraits of three species predominating. Sea kraits (*Laticauda*) differ in several ways from other sea snakes and are sometimes considered a separate family. For one thing, they often leave the water voluntarily, and one species spends so much time on land that it has a unique parasitic tick. Also, sea kraits lay eggs, while all other sea snakes are live-bearing. Female sea kraits need special conditions for rookeries, usually nesting in caves that communicate with the sea. In such places, they may congregate by the thousands.

154

Toward humans, sea kraits are exceptionally inoffensive. You can literally club one to death, and it will not try to bite. Nevertheless they have highly toxic venom. Sea kraits are the basis of fisheries in the Philippines and Ryukyu Islands. They are taken chiefly for skins, but their meat and eggs are eaten in Japan and parts of China. In 1975 the chief Philippine sea snake fishery was at Gato Island where about 50,000 snakes a month were reported taken. In Manila at that time, the Mariposa de Vida restaurant served snake dishes chiefly for their reputed aphrodisiac properties.

Sea snakes catch all their food in the sea. Many have very specialized diets; three species feed only on fish spawn and several species feed wholly or largely on eels. Our snake that made the *Guinness Book of Records* as Belcher's snake and is currently known as Cogger's sea snake feeds on garden eels. Garden eels live in burrows in dense colonies and typically are seen with most of their bodies sticking upward out of the burrow like the stem of a plant. This sea snake evidently harvests the eels by poking its small head and slender neck into the burrow, biting the eel, and swallowing it after it has been paralyzed by venom. In the Visayan Sea, we got good numbers of two very similar species of *Hydrophis*. One (*H. ornatus*) was eating a variety of fish, while the other (*H. lamberti*) seemed to be eating only marine catfish. Marine catfish have venomous spines, but we caught at least three healthy looking snakes with spines protruding through their belly wall and one with a spine protruding from the back of its head. Harold Voris found that in Malaysia, the beaked sea snake also feeds almost wholly on marine catfish. However, in Karachi I found this snake eating other fish and got one with its stomach full of prawns. On the basis of just a few observations, the big Stoke's sea snake feeds almost wholly on frogfish, which are sluggish bottom fish with venomous spines. In contrast to the specialists, the olive reef snake is a large species that eats a wide variety of fish and some invertebrates.

Around the Gigantes Islands in the Visayan Sea, we did some diving in company with local fishermen. Their air supply was pumped through hoses from a compressor in their boat rather than from a scuba tank; this is known as a hookah rig and is inexpensive, although it limits mobility and is probably

Sherman holding a sea snake on the *Alpha Helix*

more dangerous. The hookah divers ordinarily look for commercially valuable shells and coral but were glad to collect
snakes for a fee. There had been some dynamiting of the reefs
for fish and coral. Where the reefs were undamaged, the coral
was diverse and beautiful. Most of the fish were familiar types.
Lionfish, which I'd rarely seen before, were large and plentiful.
These are spectacular fish, but they have long venomous
spines. Lionfish are popular in aquariums, and I have had two
or three calls about hobbyists who have been stung. The sting
isn't fatal, but the pain is almost unendurable. Immersion of
the bitten part in water as hot as can be borne is good first aid.

At Gigantes Sur I explored a large sea cave perhaps fifty
feet high in places. It had stalactites and flowstone similar to
midwestern caves, also many bats. Swifts flew about making
clicking sounds; they had nests in the cave. In the tidal pools
were very large limpets and chitons. I'd hoped to find nests of
sea kraits but didn't; maybe it wasn't the season.

Bohol Island has an extraordinary double barrier reef, and
we anchored there several days. This was an interesting area
for our sponge and coral experts who found the reefs ecologi-
cally complex but stable. The crown-of-thorns starfish was there

but apparently wasn't doing any damage. The variety of true sea snakes was not remarkable, but two other aquatic snakes were numerous in the coastal mangroves. The file snake (*Acrochordus granulatus*) is about a yard long and has very rough, loose skin and no enlarged ventral scales. It's wholly aquatic and can live in either fresh or salt water. It can stay submerged five hours which is longer than most sea snakes can; this may be because it is very sluggish. It's nonvenomous and rarely bites. The dogfaced watersnake is a little bigger and quite ordinary looking. It's typically a snake of brackish estuaries, rarely found in the sea. It has rear fangs and presumably is somewhat venomous.

Children from the villages brought dozens of small lizards to the ship for sale or trade. Most were house geckos. The largest gecko of the area is the tokay, which can be about a foot long if its tail is complete. It has a wide range in Southeast Asia and has been introduced into southern Florida. Although it can give a painful bite, it is common in the pet trade. Its two-note call has been variously rendered as "to-kay," "tuk-koo," "toko," and "tok-tu." To American military unhappy and far from home, it sounded like "fuck you." This interpretation was so common in places that you only needed to say, "In the language of the lizard" to get your idea across.

Tamiya and I used some of the geckos to test the toxicity of sea snake venoms for reptiles. Geckos seemed to be almost as susceptible as mice on a weight-for-weight basis. On the other hand, sea snakes themselves were extremely resistant as were mangrove snakes and dogfaced watersnakes. File snakes were less resistant.

Madge had permission from the Scripps Institution of Oceanography to join the expedition in the Visayans, but because of an incredible series of misdirected, misunderstood, and undelivered messages, we missed each other at every rendezvous point. One day I took a bus across Panay Island looking for her. She was on Panay but had struck up a friendship with the Ford family who owned a large sugar mill and was their house-guest. So she was not in the hotels where I thought she might be. She finally contacted the *Alpha Helix* in Manila, but by then the expedition had ended.

Hydrophis semperi, the Lake Taal sea snake

In January 1985, Madge and I returned to the Philippines. Our contact was George Watt, a young Navy doctor stationed in Manila and interested in snakebite. He had recently reported some cases of bites by a unique snake living in Lake Taal, a volcanic crater lake in Luzon. In the center of the lake is an island that has a small lake in its center. Taal is a very active volcano. Between the time of the first Spanish records in 1572 and our visit in 1985, it had erupted forty-two times killing hundreds of people and submerging coastal villages. The Lake Taal sea snake (*Hydrophis semperi*) that has lived through all these cataclysms is one of two freshwater representatives of its family and seems restricted to this lake. File snakes also live in Lake Taal, however they are widely distributed in Asian waters. When we visited, the lake was clear and choppy. The central island of black lava and ash was sparsely covered with grass and a mesquitelike shrub. We obtained two sea snakes and a few file snakes from local fishermen. In Manila I drew blood samples from the sea snakes, and when I returned to Indiana I compared their plasma proteins with those of other Philippine sea snakes and sea snakes from other regions. My data showed the Lake Taal sea snake to be a distinct species and not a land-locked population of a marine species. This is puzzling, for there does not seem to have been enough time for it to evolve in this comparatively new lake. The alternative, which is also unlikely, is that the snake is a relict that once had a wider range but has survived only in Lake Taal.

A few days later, Dr. Watt arranged transportation for us to Lingayen Gulf where my ship the *Brooks* had been hit by a kamikaze almost exactly forty years before. On the drive up from Manila, we passed a plaque marking the base from which the kamikaze pilots took off. In the park in Lingayen city were two old Zeros covered with graffiti and political stickers.

From Manila we went to Mactan Island off the coast of Cebu. Here we had excellent snorkeling in water ten to twenty feet deep. The most spectacular creature we saw was a jellyfish about the diameter of a volleyball, sapphire blue with spikes on its bell. Its tentacles brushed my arm and shoulder giving me a good sting. Plume-worms of nine different color patterns, sea cucumbers, mushroom corals, and brain corals were conspicuous. One area was a veritable soup of salps. They look something like little jellyfish but actually are creatures intermediate between vertebrates and invertebrates. We saw many bright-colored damselfish, clown fish, and pennant fish and caught a puffer that inflated to the size of a grapefruit. Sea urchins with blue stripes and orange dots were common.

On our Caribbean trips we'd never been particularly impressed by variety of shells, but the tidal zones of Mactan, Tambuli, and Sulpa islets made up for this. Cowries, olives, cones, volutes, spider conchs, and Venus's-comb were among the types we found. There also were more kinds of starfish than I'd dreamed existed. Some had many arms in a sunburst pattern, some appeared studded with hobnails, others had arms like feathers, and others no arms at all. Under nearly every rock were long-armed, active brittle stars, harlequin crabs, and green shrimp. We caught one snake—a sea krait threaded into the rock about five feet above high tide mark.

In 1979 I got a sabbatical leave and a grant to go to Australia and study the toxicity of venoms of some of the most venomous Australian snakes for the lizards and frogs that make up a large part of the diet of these snakes. I would be working at the University of New England in Armidale where my friend, Hal Heatwole, was a member of the Zoology Department.

Australia is peculiar in having a remarkable number of highly venomous animals, the most lethal snakes and spiders, most deadly jellyfish, and the only dangerously venomous octopus, one of the few venomous mammals. Some Australians take a sort of pride in their dangerous fauna—it goes with the macho image of many Australian males. Not surprisingly, Australians have contributed a great deal to knowledge of venoms and treatment of envenomation.

In December Madge and I left for Australia. Our first stop was Guam where we stayed with Vera Cook who had been a ferry pilot with Madge during World War II. The morning after our arrival, Mrs. Cook took us on a drive around the island. On the way, I saw a large snake lying dead at the edge of the road. We stopped the car and I took a look at the reptile. It looked very much like a tree snake I'd collected in northern Australia in 1973. Mrs. Cook had lived on Guam since shortly after the war, and this was the first snake she'd seen on the island. We were seeing the dawn of an ophidian population explosion and an ecological disaster.

The brown treesnake (*Boiga irregularis*) is native to northern Australia, New Guinea, and the Bismarck and Solomon Islands. It is nocturnal and arboreal and can reach a length of almost nine feet. It is venomous, although its venom is of low toxicity for humans. Sometime about 1950 it evidently reached Guam in sea or air cargo. For the next twenty-five years or so, its numbers were small and very few persons knew it was on the island. However, about 1968 many native forest birds and bats were beginning to disappear. About ten years later snakes began to be reported regularly in populated areas, and power outages were caused by climbing snakes stretching from one electrical line to another. By 1988 nine of eleven native forest birds were extinct and three species of seabirds were virtually extinct. Rats and some species of lizards were much less common. The treesnake was unequivocally to blame, for birds, lizards, and small mammals are its food, and no other cause could be found for the decrease in so many species.

As the snakes moved closer to people, chickens and pet birds became its prey, and the number of snakebites increased markedly. Snakebites on Guam are highly unusual because many of those bitten are sleeping and often infants. In some cases, it appears the snakes were actually trying to eat the infants. Since the snake has weak venom and a relatively inefficient system for injecting it, there have been no fatalities, although a few infants have developed alarming symptoms.

Today the number of brown treesnakes on Guam seems to be decreasing due to control measures and perhaps to sheer depletion of the food supply. There is concern about the spread of the snake to other Pacific islands. Individual snakes have been found near airports in Hawaii and Saipan, but there is no proof the snakes are established on those islands.

At the time of our visit to Guam, lizards of several species were plentiful. Most of these also were recent introductions. In addition to the ubiquitous house geckos, Mrs. Cook had green anoles of the species native to the southeastern U.S. in her yard. The most plentiful lizard was a small brown skink native to Australia.

From Guam we went to Truk in the Carolines arriving shortly before Christmas. During the Pacific war, this was Japan's major island base, comparable in many ways to Pearl Harbor. In February 1944 a U.S. carrier taskforce gave Truk an unmerciful pounding. The major warships in the harbor got out, although some were sunk before they reached safety. However twenty-six large support ships—cargo ships and tenders—were sunk in Truk lagoon. Although Truk was never captured, its usefulness as a fleet base was over.

Scuba diver friends had told Madge and me of fantastic diving on the sunken ships at Truk. We'd never done much wreck diving. In the summer of 1974 we'd gone to Lake Superior with the British Sub-Aqua Club to help recover the anchor and other artifacts from the steamship *Indiana,* sunk off Crisp Point in 1858. We saw her old-fashioned steam engine and cargo of iron ore. However, at a depth of 120 feet in cold water, it was more like work than pleasure.

Truk was a different story. The reefs were not dramatically different from other Pacific reefs we'd seen, but the wrecks were. In almost thirty-six years, the huge hulls of the ships had become so covered with marine life they were hard to recognize. Some were upright, some on their sides; the tanker *Hoyo* was completely upside down. I'd never realized what huge holes torpedoes make.

Each ship we dived to told something of her story. *Heian* had been a submarine tender; in her passageways were torpedo warheads and spare periscopes, their glass lenses still clear. In the hold of the big transport *Yamagiri* were eighteen-inch shells for guns of Japan's giant battleships *Musashi* and *Yamato*. *Sankisan* was loaded with trucks and ammunition. Subchaser *Susuki* had depth charges ready on her stern. Marine organisms don't seem to grow on ceramic surfaces, so bathroom fixtures, galley tiles, and dishes looked almost as they had when the ships went down. In only one ship did I see a few human bones. Aircraft were also on the bottom of the harbor. Madge sat in the cockpit of a Mitsubishi bomber that we who served in the Pacific knew as "the Betty."

Of the marine life at Truk, the brilliantly colored soft corals were the most spectacular, but anemones, crinoids, and tunicates were in great profusion on the sunken hulks. Jellyfish were numerous, but we were beyond the range of the dangerous box-jelly. The variety of fish was as great as I've ever seen, especially on the wreck of *Fujikawa* which is in relatively shallow water. Moorish idol, rock beauty, batfish, butterfly fish, and parrot fish were among the more distinctive smaller types. Anemones and tunicates sheltered clusters of clown fish and damselfish. Large groupers and tuna and small to medium-sized sharks appeared occasionally.

On the islands around the lagoon, the massive concrete fortifications, ramps, hangars, and maintenance buildings were overgrown by jungle and looked centuries old. Large reddish purple pigeons sat in the trees, while whimbrels, phalaropes, and plovers walked about. The green skinks (*Lamprolepis*) I'd seen on many Pacific islands were common on palms outside our hotel, and we had two species of geckos in our room.

Our Australian project was an ideal one for two field her-

My association with Sherman Minton began (unknown to him) many years before we formally met. The occasion was an annual meeting of the Indiana Academy of Sciences. It was my first scientific meeting and the very first paper I heard delivered was by Sherman Minton. That meeting marked my transition from a student and amateur herpetologist into a professional biologist, and Sherman's paper was pivotal in my debut. In view of our collaboration and friendship years later, it was an appropriate ceremony.

I shared three major expeditions to study sea snakes with Sherman and he spent a sabbatical in my laboratory in Australia, working on the resistance of prey species to snake venoms. His lead in this field inspired me and years later I built upon that theme as a major focus of my own research. Some of my graduate students are continuing that work, thus maintaining continuity of a tradition that Sherman started. I was indeed touched when upon his retirement he sent me what remained of his collection of dried venoms. Behind these samples lay a story of fieldwork in far lands and the thrill of a scientific quest.

Madge and Sherman were adventurers. They enjoyed life in an intensive way, and had unbounded enthusiasm for a variety of hobbies, including diving and gem collecting. Whatever they did, they did with gusto and energy. My wife, Audry, and I have spent many happy moments with them swapping anecdotes about expeditions, fellow herpetologists, and travel. Herpetology was an obsession with them, but they knew how to balance it with many other things. I always considered Sherman to be primarily a herpetologist and often failed to remember that he was also a medical microbiologist, both in teaching and in research. That important part of his life was less evident to his herpetological colleagues and I only began to realize the full extent of his achievements as I read his memoirs. It is as though he were twins, carrying on two careers simultaneously. I admire persons who are able to broaden their horizons in this way; Sherman did it to an unusual degree.

Sherman was a considerate person. This is perhaps better illustrated by what he left out of his memoirs than by what he included. On the Chesterfield Reef expedition I was doing some blood physiology on sea snakes and had samples from a number of species on my lab bench the last day of the expedition. Sherman was also using blood to study immunological cross-reactions among different species of snakes. I had blood from one of the less common species and he had requested what was left when I finished, as he had no material from that species. I promised it to him but in the rush of the last day and under pressure to get my laboratory in order for sailing, I forgot and discarded the blood. He neither berated me (as was certainly his entitlement) nor displayed anger, but rather quietly let the matter rest. I knew how deeply disappointed he was because it made his study incomplete, and I still feel the remorse whenever I think of it. When I received the memoirs to review I turned immediately to the back to see whether he had recounted this incident. Being the gentleman he was, no mention was made.

Harold Heatwole

petologists, for we could collect snakes to serve as a source of venoms and lizards, and frogs to serve as experimental animals. We arrived at Armidale in the middle of the Australian summer and during the brief, erratic rainy season. Hal Heatwole arranged office and laboratory space for me in the zoology building and a comfortable flat for us on the campus. Armidale is a small town and the campus spread over a considerable expanse of open, rolling country. Australian magpies strolled about everywhere and awakened us with their more or less melodious whistles and cries. It was a walk of about a mile from our flat to my office, and I'd regularly see flocks of at least two species of parrots and two or three species of small lizards.

The zoology department regularly got inquiries about venomous animals. About the time we arrived, a child in a nearby town had died from the bite of a funnel-web spider, and one of my first academic activities was identifying spiders. Funnel-webs weren't common—I saw fewer than a half-dozen during my Australian sabbatical. They are big, husky spiders with large, heavy fangs. Venom of the male is more toxic than that of the female. In a series of thirteen fatal cases, male spiders caused all the deaths where the spider was available for examination. Funnel-webs seem to be basically forest creatures but adapt fairly well to living close to humans. Large adult spiders often eat small frogs. Redback spiders, related to American black widows, were plentiful in Armidale. Every house with an ornamental rock garden seemed to have a thriving population. They are about as dangerous as our black widows. Large, long-legged huntsman spiders also were common particularly under loose bark of trees. They aren't especially dangerous.

As soon as we could settle into our flat and rent a car, we started collecting in the countryside. Since it was the summer rainy season, frogs were calling wherever there was water. Some looked much like frogs you might find in Indiana but belonged to quite different families. The banjo frog (*Limnodynastes dumerilli*) looks quite a bit like the toads in Midwest gardens, and the mewing frog (*Neobatrachus pictus*) is very like a spadefoot, but both belong to the family *Leptodactylidae*, mainly native to the southern hemisphere. Australia's bell frog and

rocket frog look much like the leopard frogs that every high
school biology student used to dissect, but are more closely
related to the gray treefrog and spring peeper of the Midwest.

Snake hunting around Armidale was interesting in part
because virtually all the snakes are venomous, although not all
are dangerous. Except for the heavy, wide-headed death adder,
which was very uncommon, they are rather ordinary looking
snakes that don't have the formidable look of cobras, rattlesnakes, or puff adders. The tiger snake was the commonest
snake in the suburbs of Armidale. One I saw curled near the
front steps of a university faculty member's house was greenish gold with dark crossbands; such a handsome snake, I
watched it a moment too long and it disappeared down a hole.
A few weeks later we had a call from a man who had shot a big
tiger snake in his yard. When Madge and I arrived the snake
was still twitching. Two young snakes protruded from a hole
in its body and others could be seen moving inside. We eventually removed twenty-five, about half of them alive. We felt
they deserved a chance at life, so a few days later we released
them in good habitat far from human dwellings. Tiger snakes
like damp, grassy, open places and obviously aren't seriously
deterred by humans living near them. Tiger snakes cause
many of the serious snakebites in Australia. We kept several
in the lab. They weren't especially bad tempered, but we treated them very cautiously.

The largest snake we found near Armidale was the eastern
brown snake. One brought to the lab alive but badly injured
measured eighty inches with part of its tail missing. Madge
and Hal Heatwole encountered one at least that big at Blue
Hole, a popular picnic area. Not having equipment to capture
a snake of that size, they wisely let it go its way. Typical adult
eastern brown snakes are just what their name implies, quite
ordinary looking big brown serpents. Occasionally, however,
they may be banded, mottled, or black. We found them in various sorts of terrain, but usually where it was grassy and
open. Brown snakes are very quick and usually try to escape.
However, they will rear up and fight if cornered. One I was photographing on a patch of lawn came directly toward me with
almost half its body held off the ground. Except for another

The South Pacific and Australia

Australian land snake, the inland taipan, and one sea snake, the eastern brown snake has the most lethal venom of any snake known. But it has an extremely small venom yield for a snake its size and also very short fangs. However, some recent (1996) information indicates brown snakes now cause most of the fatalities from snakebite in Australia.

About the same size as the eastern brown snake is the red-bellied black snake, a strikingly handsome reptile that reminds me of the indigo snake of Florida. We nearly always found this snake close to water, and it was always Madge's luck to find the biggest ones when I wasn't around to catch them. This snake will rear up and flatten its neck, somewhat like a cobra. The performance seems to be mostly bluff; it is reluctant to bite. Its venom is of relatively low toxicity. We brought one large specimen back to Indianapolis where it lived several years supplying us with both blood and venom samples for our research.

A fourth dangerous snake we found regularly was the upland copperhead. While the American copperhead is well named, the Australian snake isn't. Some do have an overall dark coppery color, but I never saw one that could be described as having a copper head. This snake wasn't found close to the town, but it was almost the only snake we saw at high elevations in the forest of the Dividing Range. Its a rather placid snake, but its venom is nearly as toxic as that of the tiger snake. There were also several species of small venomous snakes seldom more than thirty inches long. It was hard to take these snakes seriously, consequently I got bitten while trying to photograph a blackbellied swamp snake (*Hemiaspis signata*). The bite wasn't very painful, but the area around the fang punctures swelled to a surprising degree, almost as if a balloon had been inflated in my finger at the knuckle. I had no other symptoms at all and the swelling disappeared in a few hours.

My most serious envenoming in Australia came from disturbing a wasp nest and getting a half-dozen or so stings on my face and neck. Those wasps, like so much of Australia's present fauna, were an introduced species. In the rain forest areas of northern Australia, land leeches are a rather spooky pest. Some patches of forest seemed covered with a moving carpet of them. It was impossible to keep them off your skin.

167

Unfed they are flat and about a half-inch long, but they quickly become little sausages as they fill with blood. In sheep- and cattle-raising areas particularly, bush flies are a plague. They don't sting or bite, but there are thousands of them, and they try to get into your eyes, nostrils, and mouth, possibly attracted by mucus. Wearing a handkerchief tied around your face like an old western bandit helps somewhat.

The kangaroo is virtually a national symbol for Australia. Kangaroos are plentiful in places, so much so that the cars of many rural Australians are equipped with "'roo bars" to minimize damage if you hit one of the beasts. I never became proficient at kangaroo identification; if it was less than four feet high, I called it a wallaby, otherwise it was a kangaroo. The gray kangaroo is the common species in the Dividing Range; we once counted about fifty in an open, grassy area. It was delightful to see them bouncing along in single file. They easily kept up with the car at a speed of 16 mph. On some of our western trips, we saw a very large animal that I suppose was the great red kangaroo. In thick undergrowth and forest, we saw smaller creatures that I presume were wallabies. And on quite a few field trips, we saw no kangaroo-like animals. Stockmen don't especially like kangaroos; several times we saw kangaroos that had been shot and their bodies hastily concealed in culverts and underbrush.

We didn't often see other marsupials. The opossum of the region around Armidale was a fluffy, gray beast that looked more like a raccoon than an Indiana possum. Bandicoots were more possumlike in general build and no smarter than a possum in getting across heavily traveled roads. Rarely, as we turned cover looking for reptiles, we'd glimpse one of the little mouselike marsupials. However, true mice, introduced by man, were extremely common in some grain-growing districts. Brown snakes and tiger snakes feed avidly on them, but apparently the snakes aren't common enough to keep rodent populations from reaching plague levels at times. Two other mammal introductions, the European rabbit and red fox, were plentiful in many places where we did field work.

Australia's most unusual vertebrates are its monotremes or egg-laying mammals. The only species we saw alive in the field was the echidna, which is about the size of a raccoon and looks like a stout porcupine with virtually no tail and a long slender snout. We found one about noon shuffling along in sparse woodland near a stream. It tried to burrow and force its way under rocks, then it curled up with its head hidden. We never saw the other monotreme, the duckbill platypus, alive, although we spent a lot of time looking for it along streams and ponds. It was said to be not especially rare near Armidale but very secretive. Our friend, John Legler, who did a lot of snorkeling in local streams as part of his turtle studies, saw them fairly regularly. Platypus males have a hollow spur on each heel connected with a venom gland in the thigh, and the animal defends itself with this weapon. There are reports of dogs having been killed and of painful but not fatal human envenoming. Monotremes are strictly protected. Madge found a large echidna dead on the road, but in excellent condition. When she brought it to the University, she was told that had she been stopped by the police, it would have been easier to explain away a human corpse than that of an echidna.

The bird life of Australia was much more evident and easily observed than the native mammals. We saw ostrichlike emus fairly regularly in the open grasslands west of Armidale, usually walking about in small groups. The galah or roseate cockatoo was very plentiful in this region, and farmers considered it a pest. In rain forest near the Queensland border, we saw another large bird, the megapod or bush turkey. It buries its eggs in mounds of decaying vegetation. The lyre bird was something of a disappointment. We saw only two of them in the mountains of the Dividing Range. As they slipped through the undergrowth, they looked like pheasants.

During my boyhood in the southern Indiana hills, waterfowl and wading birds weren't common aside from the shidepoke (little green heron), crane (great blue heron), die-dipper (pied-bill grebe), and the occasional wild ducks. So it was something of a surprise to see great numbers of such birds around the streams and ponds of the open country in the Australian highlands. The flocks of ibis were especially impressive; there also were white pelicans, cormorants, gallinules, and hundreds of ducks. In a little lake near Uralla where we hunted tiger snakes and frogs, there were black swans.

The biggest of the raptors in our part of Australia was the wedge-tailed eagle, which is about the size of the American golden eagle and similar in appearance and habits. We saw several kinds of small to moderate-sized hawks and once watched a brown falcon feeding on a galah. This falcon is also said to eat snakes frequently. Australia has no vultures, but we saw hawks feeding on road kills and other carrion several times.

Parrots are well represented in Australia. The Australian king parrot was perhaps the most spectacular species we saw, but the crimson rosella and eastern rosella are also very colorful, and the sulphur-crested cockatoo is a large and handsome species. Pigeons are also well represented, and they show greater variety in size and form than they do in North America.

The kookaburra or laughing jackass is a large kingfisher that often feeds on lizards and small snakes. We saw it frequently and heard its raucous voice even more frequently. A bird we occasionally heard in forested areas but never, with certainty, identified visually was the rifle bird or whip bird whose call is exactly like the crack of a whip or rifle. I'd always thought of wrens as sober-colored brown birds, but some of the fairy wrens of Australia are shades of brilliant blue. We saw other colorful little birds such as the red-capped finch and scarlet-breasted robin. As we were driving slowly along a road on the Atherton Plateau, a bird about the size of a song sparrow flew into our windshield. It was pleasant shades of gray spotted with gold. It seemed only stunned. After we'd taken some photos of it, it flew away. We later identified it as the diamond bird, a characteristic species of the region.

Birds weren't the only things to hit our windshield in Australia. Local road construction practices leave the pavement strewn with golfball- to baseball-sized rocks that passing trucks catapult into the front of your car. Windshield glass in 1980 was the type that shatters instantly into a million fragments that form an opaque screen before your eyes. This was highly disconcerting. Luckily the roads didn't permit really fast driving and traffic was light. After your windshield disintegrated, you stuck your head out the side window and limped into the nearest town. Every small town in the outback seemed

170

to have two places that were always busy: the pub and the garage that repaired windshields.

Mining has a long tradition in Australia. In the area where we were, gold and tin had been commercially mined, but the deposits were virtually exhausted by 1980. A few optimists panned for gold in some of the streams. Since Madge and I had panned for gold in streams of Brown County, Indiana—an activity that requires suspension of disbelief—we occasionally joined them. We got about enough gold to fill a very small cavity in a tooth but also got a few lizards and a small turtle or two. Madge had better luck sifting through gravel for precious stones. On her birthday she found a very decent sapphire that now adorns a ring.

At Lightning Ridge about 225 miles northwest of Armidale, opal mining is a major activity. We made two trips there, one in late summer (February) the other in autumn (May). The town showed a curious mixture of shiny, well-maintained trucks and mining equipment alongside ramshackle, hastily constructed dwellings. Obviously a good part of the population didn't intend to stay long. In the pub across the street from our little hotel was the "ratters' window" through which local petty thieves and con men watched for miners who might be coming in for an evening's drinking and leaving their claims unguarded.

The countryside around Lightning Ridge is dry and grassy with scattered clumps of trees and shrubs. In February it was decidedly hotter than Armidale. The amphibian and reptile fauna was considerably different. One hot afternoon as Madge and I were visiting an opal mine, we caught a large, chunky frog in the underground passage. It was one of the water-holding frogs (*Cyclorana*) that collect quantities of water in subcutaneous lymph sacs during the brief and uncertain rainy periods and then burrow to survive long dry periods. It is said aborigines know how to locate the buried frogs and use them as an emergency water source. Smaller but more colorful is the crucifix frog (*Notaden bennettii*), yellow to green with a dark cross formed by black and red warts. Its habits are like those of the water-holding frog.

The town trash dump or rubbish tip was nearly always a good spot to look for reptiles. It often retained a little moisture

171

and had a good supply of insects. This attracted lizards and some frogs. The presence of lizards and frogs attracted snakes. And the rubbish provided easily turned cover. The Lightning Ridge rubbish tip yielded several species, most interesting a shingleback or sleepy lizard curled in a heap of disintegrating rags. This is a large, stout lizard with short tail and big, heavy, overlapping scales. It looks something like a large animated pine cone and moves slowly for a lizard. It is a mild tempered omnivore. The one we caught in February gave birth to two young just before we returned to Lightning Ridge in May. We released the mother but kept the young and eventually brought them back to Indianapolis. At first they ate nothing but snails and slugs but soon shifted to a more diversified diet that included dandelion blossoms as a favorite food. They lived about twelve years with us.

Almost a hundred miles southeast of Lightning Ridge is the Pillaga Scrub, a large tract of dry forest whose chief tree is cypress pine. It has a diverse and interesting lizard fauna dominated by geckos, most of which live under loose bark of dead or damaged trees or in rock crevices. One of the most interesting is the spiny gecko (*Strophurus williamsi*), a small bluish gray lizard with rows of orange tubercles on its tail and body. Like some other snakes and lizards, it makes an open-mouthed threat gesture that exposes the intense blue lining of its mouth. Threaten it further, and it ejects from its tail strands of material much like spider silk. The stuff doesn't squirt out of the tubercles but from cracks in the skin between them. It has a faint odor somewhat like crushed maple leaves and, to my tongue, no taste at all. Others have found it has no toxicity for chickens or mice. Yet it obviously has a defensive function. My guess is that it may be directed chiefly against large spiders and centipedes and bigger lizard species that share bark crevices with the little geckos. The strong, sticky threads could impede a potential small predator enough to let the gecko escape.

The scrub is home to two very large lizards, the lace monitor, which may reach a length of almost seven feet, and the racehorse goanna, which is a bit smaller. The lace monitor is characteristic of the forest and readily climbs trees. On my sixty-first birthday, I chased a big one up a pine tree but thought twice about climbing after it. The racehorse goanna prefers open, sandy country. I don't know what its top speed is, but it's a great deal higher than mine.

Nights in the Pilliga area were hot and we cruised the almost empty roads in search of reptiles. On our first trip, I saw what appeared to be a small snake crossing the road. I got out, caught it with Pilstrom tongs, and dropped it into a bag. Madge asked what it was.

"Some sort of little elapid," I said feeling sure nearly every snake here belonged to that venomous family. A mile or two later, we caught another. When we got back to the motel, I took a closer look at them. They weren't snakes at all. As in New Guinea thirty-six years before, I'd been fooled by a pygopodid, a virtually limbless lizard. Oddly enough, pygopodids are closely related to geckos, a family that shows little limb reduction. We eventually collected three other species of pygopodids in Australia. They are the most snakelike of limbless lizards in appearance and movement. One species we caught has head and neck markings that make it an excellent mimic of young of the dangerous eastern brown snake. Some months later on another night road-cruising trip, we once again spotted what seemed to be a small snake wriggling across the pavement. This time I was pretty sure it was one of Australia's thirty or so species of blind snakes and picked it up with my fingers. It bit me, something a blind snake never does, and a closer look revealed a pair of slender legs at the base of the tail. Again I'd been fooled by an elongate lizard, this time a skink probably of the genus *Anomalopus,* although I never positively identified it. Australian skinks show nearly every possible degree of limb reduction from four perfectly good limbs to none at all.

We saw many similarities between the Australian Outback and the American West. The sheep and cattle stations were roughly equivalent to ranches. The small towns of northern New South Wales were like small towns of West Texas in the 1950s, although maybe a bit more prosperous. Many had olympic-sized swimming pools. A stay at a motel included breakfast, traditionally steak and eggs. If there was a Chinese restaurant in town, it was usually the best place to eat. Sometimes your motel gave you a chit for meals at the local servicemen's club; these meals could also be good. People were friendly and very helpful but not awfully talkative. Local language was somewhat difficult compared to American English. "The bitumen" was the blacktop road, chickens were "chooks," "amachizit" translates as "how much is it?", and "tizafta" as "this afternoon." We saw no evidence of the aboriginal culture during our travels in the outback and saw few Native Australians.

Field work was the more attractive part of our research project. In the laboratory we extracted venom from the snakes we collected and determined its lethality for the frogs and lizards that are the principal dietary items of the snakes. These snakes have unusually short fangs, so the conventional technique of hooking the fangs over the edge of a glass vial does not give a good yield of venom. Instead, Madge and I collected venom from the fang tips in thin glass tubes by capillary action. Eventually we tested venoms of the tiger snake, Australian copperhead, death adder, eastern brown snake, and redbellied black snake against thirteen species of frogs and twenty-one species of lizards. Four of these snakes have venom as toxic or more toxic for mice than venom of the Indian cobra. We injected our experimental frogs and lizards in the muscles of the hind limb. Results were surprising. Four skink species were not killed by the highest doses we injected. A White's skink weighing fifteen grams (about the weight of a small mouse) only seemed uncomfortable when injected with a dose of tiger snake venom sufficient to kill a sheep and very probably a human. Eastern brown snake venom, the second most lethal land snake venom in the world when tested on mice, killed no skink species at eighty times the dose fatal for mice nor did it kill the large bearded dragon at an even higher dose. Geckos generally showed no resistance with the exception of Tryon's velvet gecko, which was nearly as resistant as the skinks. Frogs were susceptible to the venoms, particularly those of the tiger snake and redbellied blacksnake, however the water-holding frog and the little spotted grass frog were more resistant than most of the other species we tested. There was very little evidence that venoms of the

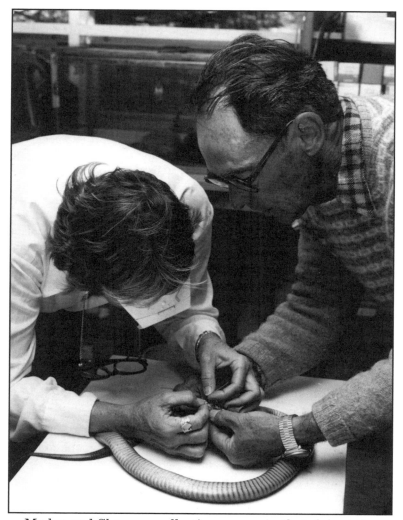

Madge and Sherman collecting venom in their lab at the
University of New England, Armidale

snakes we tested were adapted to their natural prey. All the
snakes eat skinks at least occasionally but rarely eat geckos.
Death adders and eastern brown snakes rarely eat frogs, but

they are a favorite food of tiger snakes.

Cunningham's skinks, which are highly resistant to tiger snake venom, are big enough that it's possible to get a blood sample of 0.5 cc or so from their heart without killing them. We separated their blood serum, mixed it with tiger snake venom, and injected the mixture into mice. All the mice died. So it does not seem that a natural antibody or other component of skink blood neutralizes the venom. Since neurotoxins are a major component of all these venoms, I suspect the molecular target for these toxins either doesn't exist in the resistant species or has been modified to the point where it's little affected by the neurotoxin. It's possible this has developed after thousands of years of interaction between Australian snakes and their prey.

In July 1980 at the end of my sabbatical, we joined Hal Heatwole and others on a sea snake hunt at Swain's Reefs, part of the Great Barrier Reef complex. Olive reef snakes were plentiful; we marked and released eighty-two as part of an ongoing research project. Before the snakes were released, we sometimes collected blood and venom samples. As Madge and I were using our capillary tube technique to collect venom from a large snake, the ship rolled slightly, and I impaled my finger on a fang. Sea snake bites aren't painful and don't cause swelling, so it's about an hour or two before you develop symptoms like muscle pains, stiff neck, and difficulty swallowing that indicate you've been envenomed. We had antivenin, but there seemed no point in using it prematurely. So we managed the situation, as Alistair Reid recommends, by masterly inactivity. As is the case with about two-thirds of sea snake bites, I developed no symptoms at all.

As we were diving, we had the chance to observe considerable sea snake behavior including courtship and mating. Males swam just above females, touching their backs with their tongues and chins. One pair met in midwater and coiled about each other forming a tight knot. However, they quickly separated and one investigated me closely, touching me several times. Other divers had similar experiences. Most of those intrusive snakes we caught and examined were adult males, but one that followed Madge and me about a hundred yards

The South Pacific and Australia

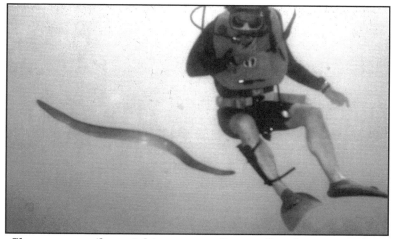

Sherman warily watching as an olive reef snake approaches

was a female. We still speculate whether the snakes were motivated by aggression, curiosity, or both. A picture she took of me as one large snake swam close to my legs indicates I thought its intention might be hostile.

The small sand cays that studded Swain's Reef were nesting areas for three species of boobies. The red-footed boobies seemed to be nesting mostly in *Messerschmidtia* shrubs while the brown and masked boobies nested on the sand. Many of the pairs had chicks almost as large as the adults. Ticks were plentiful in the bird's nests, and we found they weren't averse to feeding on humans.

The coral heads (bommies to Australians) were generally surrounded by groups of brightly colored fish, particularly chromis and humbugs. Angelfish, butterfly fish, and moorish idol also were distinctive species. Some of the larger fish such as the coral trout, footballer trout, redfin emperor, and sweetlips provided us with excellent meals. We saw a few sea turtles and small sharks. In waters around Riversong and Frigate Cays, shells were especially plentiful. I collected at least four species of cones including an exceptionally large and handsome textile cone. Cones are among the most attractive shells and those most prized by collectors. Price of the glory-of-the-seas soared out of sight in the mid-nineteenth century with a rumor that the only known locality for the species had been destroyed by an earthquake. However, other localities were discovered, and development of scuba diving proved the species to be not uncommon, although still a conchologist's prize. In 1975 when Madge visited the Ford family on Panay in the Philippines, she was allowed to hold two of the half-dozen shells in the family museum. Cone shells also can be dangerous. They have a complicated apparatus that permits them to eject a venomous dart under hydraulic pressure. The venom acts at the junction of nerve and muscle as do many snake venoms. It is mainly used to kill the fish, worms, and other shellfish on which cones feed, but it can be used in defense. There are numerous reports of shell collectors being stung and about two dozen verified fatalities. Most of the fatalities are ascribed to the geographic cone, with a small number attributed to other species including the glory of-the-seas and the textile cone. Live cone shells should be picked up only by the large end and shouldn't be carried in pockets or bags that touch the skin.

My last sea snake hunt and Australian adventure began in June 1981 in Brisbane with another expedition headed by Bill Dunson. The ship this time was the *Acheron,* a New Zealand research vessel smaller than the *Alpha Helix.* As we headed north along the Queensland coast, we were hit by a storm that did no real damage but caused considerable mess and discomfort. I was seasick for the first time in my life. After some nine hours, we gratefully dropped anchor off Heron Island, site of a well-known Australian marine biology station. Diving at Surprise Reef a few days later, I emerged from a veritable curtain of small, striped fish to see a large loggerhead turtle lying on white sand. It slowly swam off accompanied by several remoras or shark-suckers. During two days, we caught about a hundred sea snakes, nearly all olive reef snakes, and saw some beautiful parrot fish, tuskfish, and unicorn fish.

The Chesterfields are a group of tiny islands in the Coral Sea between Australia and New Caledonia. They were uninhabited in June 1981, but we found remains of old buildings and living evidence of former human settlement in the form of mice and many small geckos. Thousands of sooty terns made bedlam of Loop Islet where they had eggs and chicks in every stage of development. On Passage Islet, frigate birds with bright orange throat pouches were the dominant nesting species along with many red-footed boobies. We found dried sea snakes woven into four booby nests. Presumably the snakes were picked up dead on the beach.

The commonest sea snake was the turtlehead. I watched one probing coral crevices for fish eggs while two small fish nipped at its neck. Another common snake was the small-headed *Hydrophis* now known as Cogger's smallhead sea snake. I suspected it was an unknown species but delayed describing it, and it was described by another herpetologist. We usually saw these snakes in flat, open areas with their tiny heads and long necks poked into the burrows of small eels. Pelagic sea snakes also were plentiful. These snakes are nearly always seen at the surface, sometimes in great numbers. While other sea snakes often squirm back into the water if stranded, the pelagic sea snake seems totally helpless out of water and usually dies from overheating. Two other sea snakes we collected in the Chesterfields were the thorny-head (*Acalyptophis*) and Dubois' reef snake. Venoms of these two had never been studied. I found both to be extremely lethal for mice. In fact, Dubois' reef snake is a good contender for the "most deadly snake" title. However, there's no evidence either of these snakes has ever bitten a human. Their habitat is remote and both seem quite mild tempered.

Coral formations at our dive sites in the Chesterfields were not spectacular except for one deep reef with passages and tunnels lined with silky white gargonians. However, interesting shells including chambered nautilus, helmet shells, cowries, murex, and spider conch were fairly common. We also saw the scarlet and orange nudibranch known as Spanish dancer.

Leaving the Chesterfields, the *Acheron* headed for Saumarez and Swains Reefs. En route we saw a group of large marine animals, possibly pilot whales, some big jellyfish, probably *Cyanea,* many dolphins and flying fish. Inside the reefs the water was mirror smooth. Sea cucumbers, comb jellies, starfish, and nudibranchs were plentiful. Under the ship I saw a grouper about five feet long. Buried in the sand nearby was a large stingray. Madge arrived to spend the last two days on the reefs with me.

In Gladstone, Madge and I rented a car and headed northward in hilly, forested country. Parrots, hawks, crested pigeons, ravens, ibis, carrawongs, and other birds were numerous along the road. Night and early morning were quite chilly. This is also a mining region with chrysoprase, a green variety of chalcedony often called Australian jade, as one of its major resources. Madge bought some fine pieces of rough that eventually became interesting jewelry.

As we descended into the warmer coastal plain, we began to see bandicoots, turtles, and snakes on the road. A six-foot red-dish brown snake with a black head started across the road, disappeared under an oncoming car, and slipped off the road into a creek. I jumped into the water after it and managed to grab it. It did not seem hurt and I put it in a bag. Next day it was dead evidently from an injury inflicted by the car. It was a blackheaded python, an uncommon snake and one with dietary habits unusual for a python, since it often eats elapid snakes and apparently is immune to their venom.

For the rest of July we wandered around north Queensland, stopping at patches of rain forest on the Atherton Tableland. Here we found huge crickets and earthworms as well as several frogs and lizards we'd never seen before. Australia's rain forest also has a large green treefrog (*Litoria chloris*) with red eyes, although they are not as intensely red as those of its better known Central American relative. I've often wondered why two green treefrogs, literally a world apart, both have red eyes. We found just one live snake, an innocuous, slender tree snake about a yard long. We saw a good variety of birds, most of them unfamiliar to us. Among the more interesting were small, brightly colored birds with long beaks. They seemed to feed on nectar much like hummingbirds. The most spectacular rain forest birds were megapods or bush turkeys with orange heads. Red-browed finches and chestnut-breasted finches were common around towns as were flocks of brightly colored lorikeets.

Finally we returned to the seacoast at Cairns. Here we sat

on the beach at twilight, watched shorebirds feeding in the mud flats, and heard "Waltzing Matilda" playing somewhere in the distance. . . .

Chapter 10

Retrospective

BY H. Bernard Bechtel

Sherm did not tell anybody, even Madge, that he was writing this autobiography. She discovered the manuscript while going through his papers following his death. We do not even know if this is all he meant to include, though the last sentence, "Here we sat on the beach at twilight, watched birds feeding in the mud flats, and heard 'Waltzing Matilda' playing somewhere in the distance . . ." sounds final. If this is all that he intended, many of his accomplishments, including honors, awards, and positions of leadership, are not mentioned. Sherm was modest and I suspect too self-effacing to mention many of these things. Through conversations with Madge, along with my memories from our long friendship, I hope to fill in some of the gaps as well as to complete his story.

He retired in 1984 but remained very busy. He especially wanted to complete his revision of *Amphibians and Reptiles of Indiana,* published originally in 1972. Even without revision, his book is an outstanding example of what a state's herpetology should be, however many changes have taken place in Indiana between 1972 and now. Further collecting has demonstrated range extensions for some species, some populations have been exterminated by extensive urbanization and changes in land use, and some species previously unreported for Indiana have been discovered. For example, several populations of cottonmouth moccasins occurring in southern Indiana were not known to be there in 1972, in spite of the fact that he and numerous other herpetologists had done field work in southern Indiana. The cottonmouth is large and conspicuous, and it is somewhat astonishing that the colonies escaped notice until recently. Finally, he wanted to illustrate the revised edition in color. Since he did most of his own photography, this required extensive field work to find suitable specimens. Sherm and Madge made countless trips from one end of the state to the other. Fortunately, he discovered word processing while writing the revision, though Madge said that he frequently swore at the contraption when it would not do what he wanted it to do.

He was a member of numerous scientific organizations and a leader in most of them. He was a pioneer in the study of venomous reptiles, the toxinology of their venoms, and on the treatment of their bites, and the father of modern Hoosier herpetology. He was a former member of the Board of Governors of the American Society of Ichthyology and Herpetology; a Fellow in the Indiana Academy of Sciences, and speaker of the year in 1982; president of the International Society of Toxinology 1966-1968: and a member of the board of directors and president 1985-1986 of the Society for Study of Amphibians and Reptiles. He was the second recipient of the Redi Award (1985), the highest honor bestowed by the International Society of Toxinology.

Merely listing the organizations to which he belonged and his positions of leadership does not begin to tell what Sherman Minton meant to these organizations and to herpetology. With diverse interests, a broad and deep knowledge of general herpetology, internationally recognized expertise in venomous reptiles and their venoms, and ongoing research almost to the day he died, he was on the program too many times to list. At mixers and between sessions, he was always surrounded by a crowd of graduate students and contemporary herpetologists. He was knowledgeable, an interesting conversationalist, and above all, willing to share his knowledge and experiences, not only with herpetologists, but with amateurs. He maintained cages of living snakes on his front porch when weather permitted, and these were catnip for neighborhood boys. He patiently answered all of their questions, encouraged them if they showed any interest in herpetology, and was never condescending. I am certain that neither they nor their parents were aware of his international prominence in his field. He received many letters from young people who had discovered the world of herpetology with questions such as what courses to take in high school or college, where to look for snakes, or how to identify a specimen, and he invariably responded to them.

Sherm was a born naturalist, and he was remarkably disciplined from the outset. Among his papers are daily field notes

Sherman in his lab in Indianapolis, holding a *Pituophis*

for every year starting in 1932, when he was only thirteen. He recorded every reptile and amphibian that he encountered dead or alive, along with notes on weather and other observations. One entry, when he was sixteen and still living in New Albany, Indiana, rekindled memories of a famous weekend field trip. The following entry is from July 9, 1935: "Hiked out to the first tunnel this morning. Donald caught a pilot black snake 4 ft long near his uncle's. We saw and skinned a dead pilot black snake at Grand View. John caught a pretty little snake on the tunnel trail. I think it is a scarlet snake. Went to the show in the afternoon and loafed around the schoolyard in the evening." He did not know until later that this was the first scarlet snake reported for the state. No further specimens were found until 1957, even though the area was searched time and again by Sherm and visiting herpetologists. In 1957 we went to New Albany on a field trip. It was a cold and rainy, and did not look promising. I pried a large rock, buried halfway in the mud and not a promising site for a snake, and coiled up in a pocket beneath the rock was an adult scarlet snake. Only another herpetologist can appreciate Sherm's excitement. The following morning I turned over a flat stone and found a second specimen. His daughter, Brooks, was so frustrated that her "daddy" did not make these discoveries that she ruefully joked that Dr. Bechtel must have brought the specimens with him from Indianapolis and planted them. No further specimens have been reported, and the habitat is now so altered that they may be extinct in Indiana.

Despite the fact that Sherm and Madge had traveled over most of the world pursuing his interest in herpetology, toxinology, and medicine, he never tired of Indiana, and no wonder. It is a lovely state, from the soft hills in the south to the sloughs in the north. With its long north-south axis and variety of different habitats, it is home to a wide variety of reptiles and amphibians, there was always something to see, and he was very familiar with every part of it. He knew the location of various populations and where to go to find things. I had never seen a prairie kingsnake in the wild, for example, and asked Sherm to suggest a good site. He directed me southwest from Indianapolis on a paved highway and told me where to

Retrospective

Madge and Sherman, Brown County, Indiana, 1995

turn off on a side road and start looking. Within a few hundred feet of the highway, miraculously, a prairie kingsnake was stretched across the dirt road.

Almost from the day they married, Madge and Sherm collaborated as a team, with Madge assisting in the field, laboratory, with writing, and research on their books. It is really not possible to understand Sherm except in association with Madge. She went to all of the meetings with him and listened to countless papers and lectures. She enjoyed going to these meetings, she obviously enjoyed his company, and she was proud of his accomplishments. He was more often than not a speaker. Though she never took any courses in herpetology, she became a very knowledgeable herpetologist by listening to these lectures, as well as by her constant association with herpetology in their every activity. She was coauthor with Sherm of two books: *Venomous Reptiles* and *Giant Reptiles*.

Though we do not know how she found the time, with a family to raise in addition to all of her other activities, Madge was almost as occupied with aviation as Sherm was with herpetol-

December 1965

ogy. During World War II, slightly over 1000 young women were trained to fly military aircraft in the WASPs (Women Airforce Service Pilots), a very select group, and Madge was one of them. The WASPs were disbanded in November 1945, shortly after the war ended, though she retired before the war ended when she became pregnant with Brooks. These young lady pilots were closely bonded by their exciting adventure and formed a Retired WASP Association. Madge found time to attend their reunion, association meetings, and air shows. Though she was engrossed with aviation, Sherm looked upon airplanes only as a means of rapid transportation, and rarely accompanied her to these meetings. He did go with her to Washington for a meeting of the P-47 Pilots' Association. As Madge said, "He even attended the banquet, but spent most of his time at the Museum of Natural History talking to fellow herpetologists." In May 1991 the WASPs were invited to Russia. While Madge went to Russia, Sherm drove alone to North Carolina to collect and study salamanders. The southern Appalachians in North Carolina and Tennessee are of great interest to herpetologists, due to the abundance of salamanders, both in numbers and different species. Madge's letters to her parents during 1943–44, while she was in the WASPs, have been published and these letters leave no doubt: Madge was in love with flying then and she still is.

She is also a gem collector and a talented lapidarist, and their life style took them to many exotic markets for jewelry and artifacts and to numerous excellent gem-collecting sites. When they lived for six months in the Big Bend region of West Texas during Sherm's sabbatical leave for studying ectoparasites of reptiles, conveniently, the field next to the cabin was bountifully strewn with agate. The jewelry that Madge wears is either purchased in some exotic place or created by her.

Sherm and Madge

Madge having just found a "good" rock

enjoyed each other's company, which showed when they danced; and they did enjoy dancing. We had many meals together, both in our homes and in restaurants, and he was an adventurous eater. If he found something on a menu that he had never tasted, he generally ordered it. He was the only person I knew who could tell me what corn fungus tasted like. One thing that Sherm and Madge enjoyed together, associated with neither herpetology nor aviation, was scuba diving. They belonged to a diving club and made a number of pleasure trips to the Caribbean. Following their trip to Scotland in 1985 for Sherm to receive the Redi Award, they took a vacation to scuba dive in the Mediterranean.

Sherm and Madge shared many overseas trips not mentioned in the autobiography. In 1975 Sherm was invited to a Binational Seminar on Protein Chemistry, Snake Venoms, and Hormonal Proteins, sponsored by The National Science Foundation, USA, and the National Science Council, Republic of China, held in Taipei, Taiwan. Sherm cochaired a session on chemical and biological properties of snake venoms and presented a paper on "The Effect of Snake Venoms on Snake Erythrocytes." In 1980 he was invited to participate in an International Seminar on Epidemiology and Medical Treatment of Snakebites held in Naha, Okinawa, Japan. Sherm presented two papers. The four-day seminar allowed some time for sightseeing, but no particularly exciting field work, though Okinawa is home to some very interesting herps. While there, they were invited by the Governor of Okinawa Prefecture to a banquet in the Shuri-no-ma of Hotel Okinawa Grand Castle. Madge was especially interested in their trip to China in 1991. The Chinese Medical Association invited the Citizen Ambassador Program to organize a delegation of specialists in parasitology to exchange information with their counterparts in China. Because of his background and interests, Sherm was invited and accepted. The tour included visiting various academic and parasitology research institutions in a number of different Chinese cities. This enabled Sherm and Madge to see many of the cultural sights of China. We visited the Mintons shortly after they returned. Rather characteristic of Sherm, he had a number of slides of lizards and frogs that he had pho-

Retrospective

tographed in the grounds of a hotel, but I do not recall seeing any of the Great Wall of China.

April 12th–14th, 1996, the Indiana Academy of Sciences sponsored a symposium in honor of Sherm, starting with a reception Friday evening and ending with a field trip Sunday morning. The occasion was the publication of his second edition of his classic 1972 monograph on the amphibians and reptiles of Indiana. The event was also a reunion. Brooks, April, and Holly, along with his only grandson, April's son Benjamin, were all there. In view of the fact that Brooks lives in Mexico, the family did not often get together. The keynote address at the Friday evening dinner/reception was delivered by Whit Gibbons, professor of zoology at the University of Georgia, director of The Savannah River Ecology Laboratory, and a longtime friend of Sherm. The Saturday conference focused on the career of Sherm, and the guest speakers were individuals with whom Sherm has had personal and professional involvement. The program included presentations by David Hardy of Tucson, Arizona, Harold Voris of the Field Museum of Natural History, Carl Gans, of the Department of Biology of the University of Michigan, and me. The afternoon program focused on "Hoosier Herpetology," and consisted of eleven presentations by biologists working on the amphibians and reptiles of Indiana. Their presentations provided perspective on herpetological research in Indiana today. Sherm addressed a Saturday luncheon. I had the honor of introducing him, and had no previous knowledge of his topic, though I expected him to talk on some aspect of the herpetology of Indiana, or venomous bites by nonvenomous snakes. To my surprise, though, he presented a fascinating account of his life, describing many of the incidents that were to appear in this autobiography. His account of his last field trip with Phil Smith was most moving. Phil was terminally ill with colon cancer, and they went to one of their favorite places. They had so much in common. Phil and his wife, Dorothy, worked together much as Sherm and Madge did. Phil wrote *The Reptiles and Amphibians of Illinois,* and they did much of their field work together. This was clearly an emotional event for Sherm. I did not think about it at the time, but upon

191

Bette and Bernard Bechtel with Madge and Sherman

reflecting, it is obvious that he was writing this autobiography then, though he did not tell anybody.

More than a year after his death, Madge, Bette, and I visited Sherm's office at the Medical College, finding it as he left it. Files are bulging with papers and correspondence, and an ancient manual typewriter sits on his desk. The secretary pointed out that Sherm published more papers than any other department member. He was author or coauthor of over 150 technical papers and monographs, as well as articles in textbooks and encyclopedias, nontechnical publications, editorials, and book reviews. He typed all of his own manuscripts even though secretarial help was available. Younger readers cannot appreciate what this involved in the days before word processing. Some may have never even seen carbon paper, let alone white-out.

In November 1998 Sherm was invited to be chairman and a participant at the first Conference on Venomous Snake and Treatment for Snakebite Victims, held at Cho Ray Hospital in Ho Chi Minh City, Vietnam. Both Sherm and Madge were over eighty years old at the time, and neither had any known serious health problems, but a trip from Indianapolis to Vietnam is arduous for a person of any age. Madge was not enthusiastic about going because Sherm had been losing weight and had

Retrospective

a persistent cough, but he was insistent. The invitation was an honor. Sherm was chairman of the conference as well as a speaker, and they were the only Americans invited. She felt that he realized that this would be his final long trip, so she agreed to go. They had no problems either in the flight or while in Vietnam. They were not able to do any active field exploration, but did hire a car and driver and see the nearby countryside, and consistent with a routine that he started in 1932, Sherm was still keeping daily field notes. An entry dated 27 November 1998 is typical. "Mekong delta south of HCM City is totally flat with many ponds, canals, and river channels —water muddy. Very densely populated and intensely cultivated—rice, pineapples, bananas, jack fruit, sapodella, etc. Lotus and pink water lilies blooming along with some ornamental shrubs and vines. Predominant trees are palms and mangroves. Very little bird life. One large crane seen, plus a few smaller heronlike birds. Very few small and unfamiliar songbirds. At Mytho visited snake farm and photographed a few pythons and cobras. In moats were *Enhydris enhydris* and another *Enhydris* sp. Black with light lateral bars. Saw several, probability of 2 spp, and a *Calotes* sp. In narrow canal bordered by dense vegetation, mostly a type of palm, saw a few small mud skippers and large brown butterflies. Weather mostly overcast with a little rain in the PM."

They returned to Indianapolis exhausted by the grueling trip, and both seemed to take forever to recover. Holly and Sherm had been taking Saturday before Christmas walks for a number of years, but were able to walk for only an hour on his last Christmas. He even ceased going to the office regularly, though he remained active until March 15th. The winter of 1998–1999 was marked by an exceptionally virulent strain of flu, and they thought that this was compounding their exhaustion from the trip.

While I did not have an opportunity to talk to them at length about the trip, some of his letters give some clues. To his daughter Brooks (December 6, 1998), "Last night we arrived home and today we are recovering from jet lag and minor bouts of diarrhea, sore throat, and stiff muscles. The trip had its share of problems, mostly related to Asian Bureaucracies and

Sherman working on his specimen collection, 1994

their paperwork." To his granddaughter, Natasha (December 8, 1998), ". . . In casual dinner conversation, Madge happened to mention we'd recently celebrated our 55th wedding anniversary, and at the end of the conference we got a beautiful bouquet of flowers from the lady Minister of Health." To his friend, Dave Hardy (December 16, 1998), "I am slow in responding to your email messages because I am recovering from a bout of bronchitis I developed soon after return from Vietnam, and still feel miserable. On our trips to the Mekong delta and country around Ho Chi Minh City, we were disappointed in the scarcity of wildlife. Very few birds, lizards, even insects. Everything heavily cultivated and built up. And we had little chance to walk around on our own." Dave's history is parallel to Sherm's. He is also a physician, herpetologist, and is known nationally for snakebite treatment.

On his 80th (February 24, 1999) birthday a CAT scan was performed and it appeared that he had lung cancer, though subsequent tests suggested the possibility that the lesions were not malignant. He was feeling well enough to drive to Louisville with Madge to see *Censored on Final Approach,* a film about WASPs, and the conflicts and attitudes between

Retrospective

male and female flight personnel during World War II. This was their last outing. Following this trip he wrote the following email to his daughter Brooks (March 13, 1999), "Dearest Brooks, I thought I would pass along some more or less good news concerning my condition. Just before leaving for Louisville yesterday, I had a call about a variety of blood tests I had done about a week ago. They showed that I do not have elevated levels of antigens usually present in prostate and colon cancer which are the types most likely to show early metastases to the lungs. Everything else was pretty much normal except for a slightly elevated white blood count. So the weight of medical evidence now is that I may have some strange pulmonary infection I may or may not have picked up in Vietnam. I have been feeling generally a little better, although I still get tired easily and have lost weight but my cough is better. A few days ago we got about a 6–8 inches of snow, some of which is still on the ground. They didn't get any of this down at Louisville, and we had ideal weather for our trip down. We had a good visit with April, Ben, Kent, and all of their cats, dogs, and wildlife. Quite a variety of birds at April's feeder. Then we went to Louisville for *Censored on Final Approach,* the drama on WASPs during WWII. I found it rather overly dramatic. I don't remember anything from Madge's letters during the war that would have suggested such conflicts and attitudes between male and female flight personnel or between females, for that matter. And I don't recall that we were all that patriotic when I was at sea out in the Pacific. We wanted to get the job over and get home. Except for a few odd people like me who were fascinated with all of the strange creatures and places. After the play, Madge was asked to give some comments, which she did very tactfully. After that, we left for Indianapolis. She must have thought she was back in her flying days, for she drove straight through and got us home about 2 AM. Love, Daddy"

This last comment by Sherm referred to Madge's legendary (some would call it hair-raising) driving. She had flown P-47 fighters for the WASPs during World War II, and her friends were all certain that she drove her cars exactly the way she handled the P-47s; and it was not only her friends who noted these driving tendencies. The June 1999 issue of *Life* magazine contains a feature article about Madge entitled "The Fly Girl." To establish background material for the article, a photographer was assigned to visit the Mintons in Indianapolis, and after riding with Madge she included the following in the *Life* article, "In her little old tin can of a car, she grips the wheel with knobby fingers, and battles a rainstorm on the Indiana highway. The car is lashed by the wakes of passing trucks, and the wipers can't keep up—they're shoving plates of water from side to side. Visibility's zero, she's going 70, she's nearly 80, so naturally Madge Rutherford Minton steps on the gas."

Sherm's driving could be a little scary too. Except on busy interstates, he invariably came to a screeching halt when he saw any live or dead reptile or amphibian on the highway, and he had a good eye for them. If the specimen was already dead, the stop entailed pulling to the side of the road while he preserved the specimen and recorded the time, place, weather, and all pertinent data. If it was alive, he would collect it if he had any reason, or more likely place it well off the side of the highway.

March 15th he was admitted to IU Hospital because of convulsions due to cranial metastases. Symptomatic therapy, including out-patient radiation to cranial lesions, was of minimal benefit. The physician advised the family that Sherm had at most several months to live. He died June 15, 1999, at a hospice. Both Madge and Holly commented on the peculiar timing of the death of Sherm's black cat, named Abuzarid. "Abu" came to the Mintons as a stray in 1980, and his favorite resting place was on Sherm's lap. On June 14th, Madge placed him in a cat carrier to take him to the veterinarian. She stopped on the way for a brief visit with Sherm, and when she returned to the car, "Abu" was dead. Madge told Holly, "The cat died to show Sherm the way." Shortly before Sherm was admitted to a hospice center, we visited him. The last night of the visit we propped him on the sofa and he showed us a series of slides from Mexico that he had assembled for a lecture. Since Brooks lived in Mexico, the Mintons went there frequently and Sherm was familiar with both the culture and the herpetofauna.

Sherm had left no written instructions, but when he knew

Retrospective

Sherman with Rufus in 1987

he was dying, he gave explicit instructions to Madge which she courageously carried out. Madge told me that some of her friends asked her if she actually carried out these instructions. Well, she did. With his ashes in an urn, she drove alone to Corydon, a picturesque small town in southern Indiana, and the first capitol of Indiana. She met Mike and Patti Lodato, friends from Evansville, and they spent the evening at the Kintner House Bed and Breakfast. The following morning they drove to the Mosquito Creek Nature Preserve in Harrison County, a tranquil place characteristic of the southern Indiana hill country that Sherm so loved. Where Mosquito Creek empties into the Ohio River, Madge scattered Sherm's ashes over the water. Flowers were placed on the water and, as they floated to the Ohio River, the three drank wine that Mike had brought for the occasion, and Madge, Mike, and Patti wished Sherm a happy journey.

THE PUBLICATIONS OF SHERMAN A. MINTON, JR.

1942 (with L.A. Weed & E. Carter) **Specificity of the lecithovitellin reaction in diagnosis of gas gangrene due to *Clostridium welchii*.** War Medicine 2:952–959.

1943 (with L.A. Weed) **Non-specificity of serum opacity test for *Clostridium welchii*.** Journal of Laboratory and Clinical Medicine 28:1251–1253.

1944 **Introduction to the study of the reptiles of Indiana.** American Midland Naturalist 36:912–974.

1947 **An annotated list of herpetological papers from the Proceedings of the Indiana Academy of Science.** Herpetologica 3:195–202.

1948 (with J.E. Minton) **Notes on a herpetological collection from the middle Mississippi Valley.** American Midland Naturalist 40:378–390.

1949 (with Hobart M. Smith & C.W. Nixon) **Observations on the constancy of color and pattern in soft-shelled turtles.** Transactions of the Kansas Academy of Science 1:92–98.

1949 **The black-headed snake in southern Indiana.** Copeia 1949:146–147.

1949 **An ectopic egg in *Coluber*.** Herpetologica 5:186.

1950 **Injuries by venomous animals in Indiana.** Proceedings of the Indiana Academy of Science 60:315–321.

1951 **Isolation of Coxsackie virus from a case of suspected poliomyelitis.** Quarterly Bulletin of the

Indiana University Medical Center 13:3–6.
1951 **Know your snakes.** Outdoor Indiana, April.
1951 (with R.L. Thompson & M.L. Price) **Protection of mice against vaccinia virus by administration of benzaldehyde thiosemicarbazone.** Proceedings of the Society for Experimental Biology and Medicine 78:11–13.
1951 (with R.L. Thompson, M.L. Price, E.A. Falco & G.H. Hitchings) **Protection of mice against the vaccinia virus by administration of phenoxythiouracils.** Journal of Immunology 67:483–491.
1952 **Isolation of a pox virus from human source.** Quarterly Bulletin of the Indiana University Medical Center 14:14–17.
1952 **Snakebite in the Midwestern region.** Quarterly Bulletin of the Indiana University Medical Center 14:1–4.
1953 (with R.L. Thompson & J.E. Officer) **Effect of thiosemicarbazones and dichlorophenoxythiouracil on multiplication of a recently isolated strain of the variola-vaccinia virus in the brain of the mouse.** Journal of Immunology 70:222–228.
1953 (with R.L. Thompson, J.E. Officer & G.H. Hitchings) **Effect of heterocyclic and other thiosemicarbazones on vaccinia infection in the mouse.** Journal of Immunology 70:228–234.
1953 **Common reptiles of the Midwest.** Conservation Cavalcade, June.
1953 **Variation in venom samples from copperheads and timber rattlesnakes.** Copeia 1953:212–215.
1953 **Salamanders of the *Ambystoma jeffersonianum* complex in Indiana.** Herpetologica 10:173–179.
1954 **Polyvalent antivenin in the treatment of experimental snake venom poisoning.** American Journal of Tropical Medicine and Hygiene 3:1077–1082.
1954 (Book review) **The Frogs, Toads and Salamanders of Eastern Canada by E.B.S. Logier, Clarke Irwin, Toronto, 1952.** Copeia 1954:76.
1955 **The trap-door spider *Pachylomerides adouinii***

The Publications of Sherman A. Minton, Jr.

in southern Indiana. Proceedings of the Indiana Academy of Science 64:255.

1955 **Some health problems for the medical zoologist in the Big Bend country of Texas.** Quarterly Bulletin of the Indiana University Medical Center 16:34–37.

1956 **A new snake of the genus *Tantilla* from west Texas.** Fieldiana Zoology 34:449–452.

1956 **Some properties of North American pit viper venoms and their correlation with phylogeny.** pp. 145–151 *In:* Venoms (E.E. Buckley & N. Porges, eds.) American Association for the Advancement of Science, Washington, D.C.

1957 **Snakebite.** Scientific American 196:113–114.

1957 **An immunological investigation of rattlesnake venoms by the agar diffusion method.** American Journal of Tropical Medicine and Hygiene 6:1097–1103.

1957 **Variation in yield and toxicity of venom from a rattlesnake *Crotalus atrox*.** Copeia 1957:265–269.

1957 (with P.W. Smith) **A distributional summary of the herpetofauna of Indiana and Illinois.** American Midland Naturalist 59:241–251.

1958 (with H.B. Bechtel) **Another Indiana record of *Cemophora coccinea* and a note on egg-eating.** Copeia 1958:47.

1959 **Observations on the amphibians and reptiles of the Big Bend region of Texas.** Southwestern Naturalist 3:28–54.

1959 **Venomous animals, spiders, and insects.** Pest Control 27:23–30.

1960 (with H.M. Smith) **A new subspecies of *Coniophanes fissidens* and notes on Central American amphibians and reptiles.** Herpetologica 16:103–111.

1960 (with Madge R. Minton) **Additional records of the eastern spadefoot from Indiana.** Herpetologica 16:259.

1960 **Notes from a Pakistan herpetological diary.**

Bulletin of the Philadelphia Herpetological Society 1960, pp. 21–24.

1961 **Adder.** Encyclopedia Britannica 1961, vol. 1, p. 131.

1961 **Black Snake.** Ibid., vol. 3, p. 748.

1961 **Venom.** Ibid., vol. 23, pp. 69–70.

1962 **An annotated key to the amphibians and reptiles of Sind and Las Bela, West Pakistan.** American Museum Novitates No. 2081:1–60.

1962 (with J.A. Anderson) **A record of the turtle *Hardella thurgi* from salt water.** Herpetologica 18:126.

1963 **Snakebite.** pp. 1797–1802 *In:* Cecil Loeb Textbook of Medicine, 11th ed. (P.B. Beeson & W. McDermott, eds.) Saunders, Philadelphia.

1963 (with J.A. Anderson) **Two noteworthy records from the Thar Parkar desert, West Pakistan.** Herpetologica 19:152.

1963 (with J.A. Anderson) **Feeding habits of the kukri snake, *Oligodon taeniolatus*.** Herpetologica 19:147.

1963 **Bats, rabies, and spelunking.** Bloomington Indiana Grotto Newsletter (2):30–31.

1964 (with Madge R. Minton) **The snake charmers of Sind.** Bulletin of the Philadelphia Herpetological Society 1964:35–38.

1964 (with Charlotte Olson) **A case of spider bite with severe hemolytic reaction.** Pediatrics 33:154–155.

1964 (with J.A. Anderson) **A new dwarf gecko from Baluchistan.** Herpetologica 21:59–61.

1964 (Book review) (with Herndon Dowling) **Poisonous Snakes of the World** (Medical Unit, Office of Naval Intelligence), Govt. Printing Office, Washington, 1963. Copeia 1964:458–459.

1964 (Book review) **Die Giftschlangen der Erde Behringwerke, Marberg-Lahn,** 1963. Copeia 1964:595.

1965 (with E.V. Malnate) **A redescription of the natracine snake *Xenochrophis cerasogaster* with comments on its taxonomic status.** Proceedings of the Academy of Natural Sciences in Philadelphia 117:19–43.

The Publications of Sherman A. Minton, Jr.

1965 (Book review) **Bibliography of Snake Venoms and Venomous Snakes by F.E. Russell & R.S. Scharffenberg, Bibliographic Assoc., West Covina, CA, 1964.** Copeia 1965:260.

1965 (Book review) **¿Qué sabe usted de viboras? by J. Abalos, Libros Caminante, Buenos Aires, 1964.** Toxicon 3:73.

1966 **A Contribution to the Herpetology of West Pakistan.** Bulletin of the American Museum of Natural History 134:31–184.

1966 **Amphibians and reptiles (of Indiana).** pp. 426–451 *In:* Natural Features of Indiana (A.A. Lindsey, ed.) Indiana Academy of Science, Indianapolis.

1966 (with M.A. Haleem) **The effects of adrenalectomy and splenectomy on *Trypanosoma lewisi* infection in white rats.** Journal of Tropical Medicine and Hygiene 69:294–298.

1966 **Snakebite—what to do in case of . . .** Indiana State Board of Health Bulletin 39:8–11.

1966 (Book review) **Poisonous Snakes of the Eastern United States by H.T. Davis, North Carolina State Museum, Raleigh.** Copeia 1966:627.

1967 **Observations on toxicity and antigenic makeup of venoms from juvenile snakes.** pp. 211–222. *In:* Animal Toxins (F.E. Russell & P.R. Saunders, eds.) Pergamon Press, Oxford.

1967 **Marine venoms.** p. 425 *In:* Cecil Loeb Textbook of Medicine (P.B. Beeson & W. McDermott, eds.) Saunders, Philadelphia.

1967 **Paraspecific protection by elapid and sea snake antivenins.** Toxicon 5:47–55.

1967 (Book review) **Poisonous Snakes of Southern Africa . . . by J. Visser, Timmins, Capetown, 1966.** Copeia 1967:498–499.

1968 **Antigenic relationships of the venom of *Atractaspis microlepidota* to that of other snakes.** Toxicon 6:59–64.

1968 **Venoms of desert animals.** pp. 487–516 *In:* Desert Biology (G.W. Brown Jr., ed.) Academic Press, New York.

1968 **Preliminary observations on the venom of Wagler's pit viper.** Toxicon 6:93–97.

1968 **Copperhead. Cottonmouth. Death adder. Jararaca.** Encyclopedia Americana.

1968 (with Allan Roberts) **Zur Fortpflanzung von *Sceloporus formosus*.** Salamandra 4:1–3.

1968 **Obituary: Laurence M. Klauber, 1883–1968.** Toxicon 6:159–160.

1968 **The fate of amphibians and reptiles in a suburban area.** Journal of Herpetology 2:113–116.

1968 (Book review) **Venomous Animals and their Venoms (W. Bucherl, E.E. Buckley & V. Deulofeu, eds.) Vol. I, Venomous Vertebrates, Academic Press, New York, 1968.** Copeia 1968:885–886.

1969 (with Sylvia Kendall) **Serum profiles of certain reptile sera and preliminary observations on antibody formation in snakes.** Proceedings of the Indiana Academy of Science 78:113–114.

1969 (with Madge R. Minton) **Venomous Reptiles,** Scribners, New York, xii + 273 pp.

1970 **The feeding strike of the timber rattlesnake.** Journal of Herpetology 3:121–124.

1970 (with S.C. Anderson & J.A. Anderson) **Remarks on some geckos from southwest Asia with descriptions of three new forms and a key to the genus *Tropiocolotes*.** Proceedings of the California Academy of Science 37:333–362.

1970 **Dr. Goethe Link—Herpetologist.** Journal of the Indiana State Medical Association 63:766–767.

1970 **Snake venoms and envenomation.** Clinical Toxicology 3:343–345.

1970 **Identification of poisonous snakes.** Clinical Toxicology 3:347–362.

1971 **Venom diseases.** pp. 76–82 *In:* Cecil Loeb Textbook of Medicine (P.B. Beeson & W. McDermott, eds.) 13th ed. Saunders, Philadelphia.

1971 (Editor) **Snake Venoms and Envenomation.** Marcel Dekker, New York, ix + 188 pp.

1971 **Indiana turtles: distribution and present status**

The Publications of Sherman A. Minton, Jr.

of populations. Proceedings of the Indiana Academy of Science 80:485–486.

1971 **Snakebite—an unpredictable emergency.** Journal of Trauma 11:1053.

1971 (Book review) **Reptiles of Oklahoma by R.G. Webb, University of Oklahoma Press, Norman, 1970.** Quarterly Review of Biology 46:310.

1971 (Book review) **The Last of the Ruling Reptiles by W.T. Neill, Columbia Univ. Press, New York, 1971.** Herpetological Review 3:113.

1972 **Poisonous spiders of Indiana and report of a bite by *Chiracanthium mildei*.** Journal of the Indiana State Medical Association 65:425–426.

1972 (with Sylvia K. Salanitro) **Serological relationships among some colubrid snakes.** Copeia 1972:246–252.

1972 **Amphibians and Reptiles of Indiana.** Indiana Academy of Science, Indianapolis, v + 346 pp.

1973 (with Madge R. Minton) **Giant Reptiles.** Scribners, New York, xiii + 345 pp.

1973 (with C.A. Bonilla & M.R. Faith) **L-amino acid oxidase, phosphodiesterase, total protein and other properties of juvenile timber rattlesnake venom at different stages of growth.** Toxicon 11:301–304.

1973 (Book review) **Venomous Animals and their Venoms (W. Bucherl & E.E. Buckley, eds.) Vol. II, Venomous Vertebrates, Academic Press, New York, 1971.** Copeia 1973:386–387.

1973 (with Harold Heatwole et al.) **Arboreal habits in Australian elapid snakes.** HISS News Journal 1:113.

1973 **Common antigens in snake sera and venoms.** pp. 903–917 *In:* Toxins of Animal and Plant Origin (A. deVries & E. Kochva, eds.) Gordon & Breach, New York, Vol. 3.

1973 (with S.K. Salanitro) **The immune response of snakes.** Copeia 1973:504–513.

1974 Introduction to **The Bulletin of the Antivenin Institute of America,** reprint ed. Society for the Study of Amphibians and Reptiles, Oxford, OH, pp. iii–v.

1974 **Venom Diseases.** Charles C. Thomas, Springfield, IL, xv + 235 pp.

1974 Introduction to **Venomous Animals of the World** by Roger Caras. Prentice Hall, Engelwood Cliffs, NJ, pp. vii–ix.

1975 **Venomous marine invertebrates.** pp. 1031–1036 *In:* Diseases Transmitted from Animals to Man (W.T. Hubbert, W.F. McCulloch & P.R. Schnurrenberger, eds.) 6th ed. Charles C. Thomas, Springfield, IL.

1975 **Venomous arthropods.** Ibid., pp. 1037–1050.

1975 **Venomous vertebrates.** Ibid., pp. 1051–1059.

1975 **Parasitism by miscellaneous invertebrates.** Ibid., pp. 1060–1072.

1975 **A note on the venom of an aged rattlesnake.** Toxicon 13:73–74.

1975 **Observations on sea snakes at Ashmore Reef, Timor Sea.** Proceedings of the Indiana Academy of Science 83:467–468.

1975 (with H.G. Dowling) **Snakebite.** HISS Yearbook of Herpetology 1:213–218.

1975 **Geographic distribution of sea snakes.** pp. 21–31 *In:* The Biology of Sea Snakes (W.A. Dunson, ed.) University Park Press, Baltimore.

1975 (with M.S. da Costa) **Serological relationships of sea snakes and their evolutionary implication.** Ibid., pp. 33–55.

1975 (with Harold Heatwole) **Sea snakes from three reefs of the Sahul Shelf.** Ibid., pp. 141–144.

1975 **Snakebite in zoos.** International Zoo Yearbook 15:179–191.

1975 (with M.R. Minton) Geographic distribution: *Hemidactylus mabouia.* Herpetological Review 6:116.

1975 (with B.M. de Cervantes) Geographic distribution: *Coniophanes frangivirgatus.* Ibid. 6:116.

1975 (with B.M. de Cervantes) Geographic distribution: *Micrurus fulvius.* Ibid. 6:116.

1975 (with B.M. de Cervantes) Geographic distribution: *Typhlops braminus.* Ibid. 6:117.

The Publications of Sherman A. Minton, Jr.

1975 (Book review) **Husbandry, Medicine and Surgery in Captive Reptiles by F.L. Frye, VM Publishing, Bonner Springs, KS, 1973.** Copeia 1975:388.

1976 **Snakebite revisited.** Indiana State Board of Health Bulletin 78:15–16.

1976 **The effect of snake venoms on snake erythrocytes** (abstract). U.S.-Republic of China Seminar on Protein Chemistry, Taipei, Taiwan, 1976. Reprinted, Toxicon 14:413.

1976 (with J.D. Fix) **Venom extraction and yields from the North American coral snake *Micrurus fulvius*.** Toxicon 14:143–145.

1976 **Neutralization of Old World viper venoms by American pit viper antivenin.** Toxicon 14:146–148.

1976 **Serological relationships among some congeneric American and Eurasian colubrid snakes.** Copeia 1976:672–678.

1977 **Spines, stings, and sea snakes.** Consultant 17:45–63.

1977 (with Brooks M. de Cervantes) **Observations on the snakes of Queretaro, Mexico.** Bulletin of the Chicago Herpetological Society 12:69–74.

1977 **Toxicity of venoms from some little known Mexican rattlesnakes.** Toxicon 15:580–581.

1977 (Book review) **Venoms: Chemistry and Molecular Biology by A.T. Tu, John Wiley, New York, 1977.** American Journal of Pharmaceutical Education 41:552.

1978 **Serological relationships of some Philippine sea snakes.** Copeia 1978:151–154.

1978 (with H. Heatwole) **Snakes and the sea.** Oceans 11(2):53–56.

1978 (with W.A. Dunson) **Observations on the Palawan mangrove snake, *Boiga dendrophila multicincta*.** Journal of Herpetology 12:107–108.

1978 (with W.A. Dunson) **Diversity, distribution and ecology of Philippine marine snakes.** Journal of Herpetology 12:281–286.

1978 (with N. Tamiya & C. Takasaki) **Toxicity of sea snake venoms for amphibians and reptiles** (abstract) pp. 434–435 *In:* Toxins: Animal, Plant, and Microbial (P. Rosenberg, ed.) Pergamon Press, Oxford.

1978 (with D. Mebs) **Vier Bissfalle durch Colubriden.** Salamandra 14:41–43.

1978 **Beware: nonpoisonous snakes.** Natural History 87:56–60.

1978 **If your own skin doesn't taste good, try someone else's.** Bulletin of the Chicago Herpetological Society 13:49.

1978 (with F.E. Russell) **Poisonous snakes: I & II.** Clinical Medicine 85(11):11–22.

1978 (with F.E. Russell & C. Gans) **Poisonous snakes: III–V.** Ibid. 85(12):13–30.

1978 **Serological relationships among some midwestern snakes.** Proceedings of the Indiana Academy of Science 87:438–445.

1978 (with H. Heatwole, Ron Taylor & Valerie Taylor) **Underwater observations on sea snake behaviour.** Records of the Australian Museum 31:737–761.

1979 **Common antigens in snake venoms.** *In:* Snake Venoms (C.Y. Lee, ed.) Handbook of Experimental Pharmacology 52:847–862.

1979 **Who gets bitten by snakes and why.** Bulletin of the Chicago Herpetological Society 14:67–72.

1979 (Book review) **Biology of the Reptilia, Vol. 8: Physiology B (Carl & K.A. Gans, eds.) Academic Press, London & New York, 1978.** Quarterly Review of Biology 54:466.

1979 **Beware: nonpoisonous snakes.** Clinical Toxicology 15(3):259–265.

1980 (with Madge R. Minton) **Venomous Reptiles, revised edition.** Scribners, New York, xii + 308 pp.

1980 ***Thamnophis butleri.*** Catalogue of American Amphibians and Reptiles (258):1–2.

1980 **Snakebites in the U.S.A.** (abstract) International Seminar on Epidemiology and Medical Treatment of Snakebites, Okinawa, p. 141.

1980 **Paraspecific neutralization by antivenoms.** (abstract) Ibid., p. 165.

The Publications of Sherman A. Minton, Jr.

1981 **Evolution and distribution of venomous snakes.** pp. 55–59 *In:* (C.B. Banks and A.A. Martin, eds.) Proceedings of the Melbourne Herpetological Symposium. Royal Melbourne Zoological Gardens, Australia, 19–21 May 1980. Zoological Board of Victoria, Melbourne.

1981 **Not just another pretty face.** Animal Kingdom 84:31–35.

1981 (with Madge R. Minton) **Toxicity of some Australian snake venoms for potential prey species of reptiles and amphibians.** Toxicon 19:749–755.

1982 **Snake Bite.** pp. 283–300 *In:* Parasitic Zoonoses, Vol. 3 (J.H. Steele, ed.) CRC Press, Boca Raton, FL.

1982 (Book review) **Survey of Contemporary Toxicology, Vol. 2 (A.T. Tu, ed.), John Wiley, Somerset, NJ, 1982.** American Journal of Tropical Medicine and Hygiene 32:1299.

1982 (Book review) **Rattlesnake Venoms, their Action and Treatment (A.T. Tu, ed.) Marcel Dekker, New York, 1982.** Herpetologica 38:273–74.

1983 **Cottonmouth.** Outdoor Indiana 48:14–19.

1983 *Sistrurus catenatus.* Catalogue of American Amphibians and Reptiles (332):1–2.

1983 **Arthropod envenomation.** pp. 270-304 *In:* Management of Wilderness and Environmental Emergencies (P.S. Auerbach & E.C. Geehr, eds.) Macmillan, New York.

1983 (with A.B. Wilson) Geographic distribution: *Agkistrodon piscivorus leucostoma.* Herpetological Review 14:34.

1983 **Lethal toxicity of venoms of snakes from the Coral Sea.** Toxicon 21:901–902.

1983 (Book review) **Rattlesnakes: their Habits, Life Histories, and Influence on Mankind by L.M. Klauber (abridged edition) University of California Press, Berkeley, 1982.** Quarterly Review of Biology 58:103–104.

1984 **The knob country remembered.** Notes from NOAH (Northern Ohio Association of Herpetologists) 11:45–49.

1984 **Highlights in herpetology: it's not all snakes.** Proceedings of the Indiana Academy of Science 92:70–76.

1984 (with J.C. List & M.J. Lodato) **Recent records and status of amphibians and reptiles in Indiana.** Proceedings of the Indiana Academy of Science 92:489–498.

1984 (Book review) **Venomous Snakes of the World. A Checklist by K.A. Harding & K.R.G. Welch, Pergamon Press, Oxford, 1980.** Toxicon 22:326.

1984 (with S.A.Weinstein) **Lethal potencies and immunoelectrophoretic profiles of venoms of *Vipera bornmulleri* and *Vipera latifii*.** Toxicon 22:625–629.

1984 (with Madge R. Minton) Geographic distribution: *Anolis sagrei*. Herpetological Review 15:77.

1984 (with S.A. Weinstein) **Immunodetection of North American pit viper venoms** (abstract). XI International Congress on Tropical Medicine & Malaria, p. 101.

1984 (with S.A. Weinstein) **Protease activity and lethal toxicity of venoms of some little known rattlesnakes.** Toxicon 22:828–830.

1984 (with S.A. Weinstein & C.E. Wilde) **An enzyme-linked immuno-assay for detection of North American pit viper venoms.** Journal of Toxicology and Clinical Toxicology 22:303–316.

1985 **Letter to editor: Antivenin dosage.** Journal of Trauma 25:464.

1985 **Letter to editor: The shifting sands of nomenclature.** Toxicon 23:186.

1985 (with S.A. Weinstein & C.E. Wilde) **The distribution among ophidian venoms of a toxin isolated from the venom of the Mojave rattlesnake *(Crotalus s. scutulatus)*.** Toxicon 23:825–844.

1985 (with W.A. Dunson) **Sea snakes collected at Chesterfield Reefs, Coral Sea.** Atoll Research Bulletin (292):101–108.

1986 (with S.A. Weinstein) **Geographic and ontogenic variation in venom of the western diamondback rattlesnake *(Crotalus atrox)*.** Toxicon 24:71–80.

1986 **Venomous bites by "nonvenomous" snakes.** Wilderness Medicine 3:6–7.

The Publications of Sherman A. Minton, Jr.

1986 **Vipers, rattlesnakes, and cobras.** pp. 130–131 *In:* The Encyclopedia of Reptiles and Amphibians (T. Halliday & K. Adler, eds.) Equinox Ltd., Oxford.

1986 **Origins of poisonous snakes: evidence from plasma and venom proteins.** pp. 3-21 *In:* Natural Toxins: Animal, Plant, and Microbial (J.B. Harris & D.S. Chapman, eds.) University Press, Oxford.

1987 **Comment on electric shock treatment of snakebites.** Wilderness Medicine 4(2):4.

1987 **Poisonous snakes and snakebite in the U.S.: a brief review.** Northwest Science 61:130–137.

1987 (Book review) **Atlas of Elapid Snakes of Australia (R. Longmore, ed.), Australian Government Publishing Service, Canberra, 1986.** Toxicon 22:326.

1987 **Present tests for detection of snake venom: clinical applications.** Annals of Emergency Medicine 16:932–937.

1987 **In memoriam: Philip W. Smith.** Herpetological Review 18:48.

1987 (with S.A. Weinstein) **Colubrid snake venoms: immunologic relationships, electrophoretic patterns.** Copeia 1987:993–1000.

1988 (with Sarbelio Moreno) *Geophis* **sp. predation.** Herpetological Review 19:35.

1988 (with J.G. Soto & J.C. Perez) **Proteolytic, hemorrhagic and hemolytic activities of snake venoms.** Toxicon 26:875–890.

1988 **Reptiles of the Pakistan deserts.** pp. 99–164 *In:* Ecophysiology of Desert Vertebrates (P.K. Ghosh & I. Prakash, eds.) Scientific Publishers, Jodhpur, India.

1989 **Snakebite.** pp. 1023–1026 *In:* Conn's Current Therapy (R.B. Rakel, ed.) Saunders, Philadelphia.

1989 (with H.B. Bechtel) **Arthropod envenomation and parasitism.** pp. 514–541 *In:* Management of Wilderness and Environmental Emergencies 2nd ed. (P.S. Auerbach & E.C. Gheer, eds.) Mosby, St. Louis.

1989 (with J.G. Soto, J.C. Perez, M.M. Lopez, M. Martinez, T.B. Quintanila-Hernandez, M.S. Santa-Hernandez, K. Turner, J.L. Glenn, and R.C. Straight) **Comparative** enzymatic study of HPLC-fractionated *Crotalus* venoms. Comparative Biochemistry and Physiology 93B (4):847–855.

1989 (Book review) **The Biology of Australasian Frogs and Reptiles (G. Grigg, R. Shine & H. Ehmann, eds.) Surrey, Beatty & Sons, Chipping Norton, NSW, 1985.** Herpetological Review 20:24–25.

1989 (Book review) **Gray's Monitor Lizard by W. Auffenberg, University of Florida Press, Gainsville, 1988.** Herpetological Review 20:24.

1989 (Book review) **Francesco Redi on Vipers by Peter Knoefel, E.J. Brill, Leiden, 1988.** Herpetological Review 20:56.

1989 (Book review) **The Isle of Sea Lizards by Angus Bellairs, Durrell Institute Conservation & Ecology, Canterbury, 1989.** Herpetological Review 20:100.

1990 **Neurotoxic snake envenoming.** Seminars in Neurology 10:52–61.

1990 **Venomous bites by nonvenomous snakes: an annotated bibliography of colubrid envenomation.** Journal of Wilderness Medicine 1:119–127.

1990 (Book review) **Australian Reptiles and Frogs by R.T. Hoser, Pierson & Co., Sydney, 1989.** Herpetological Review 21:97–98.

1990 **Snake that kill people. The Asian cobras.** The Monitor 2(3):2–3.

1990 **Saw-scaled vipers.** Ibid. (4):1–3.

1990 **Russell's viper.** Ibid. (5):1–2.

1990 **Neotropical lanceheads.** Ibid. (6):1–3.

1990 **Puff adder.** Ibid. (7):1–2.

1990 **The Rattlesnakes.** Ibid. (8):1–3.

1990 **Poisonous snakes of the Middle Eastern war zone.** Sonoran Herpetologist 3:87–90.

1990 **Scientific collecting, voucher specimens and things like that.** The Monitor 2(9):1–3.

1990 **Clinical hemostatic disorders caused by venoms.** pp. 518–531 *In:* Disorders of Hemostasis (O.D. Ratnoff & C.D. Forbes, eds.) Saunders, Philadelphia.

The Publications of Sherman A. Minton, Jr.

1990 **Immunologic relationships in *Agkistrodon* and related genera.** pp. 589–600 *In:* Snakes of the *Agkistrodon* Complex (H.K. Gloyd & R. Conant) Society for the Study of Amphibians and Reptiles, Oxford, OH.

1991 (with Madge R. Minton) ***Masticophis mentovarius* (Neotropical Whipsnake) reproduction.** Herpetological Review 22:100–101.

1991 (Book review) **Snakes of Iran by M. Latifi. (Translated by Sepideh Sajadian; A. Leviton & G. Zug, eds.) Society for the Study of Amphibians and Reptiles, Oxford, OH, 1991.** Herpetological Review 22:136.

1991 **Relationships of east Asian venomous snakes: evidence from venom and plasma proteins** (abstract). Second International Meeting on Tropical Medicine and Parasitology, Hainan, China, pp. 149–150.

1991 **Bonaire: an island of lizards.** The Monitor 3(8):1–2.

1991 (with Madge R. Minton) **Rattlesnakes and Mexican folk medicine.** Herpetological Review 22:116.

1992 **Reptiles as a source of human infections.** pp. 3–7 *In:* Greater Cincinnati Herpetological Society Contributions in Herpetology (P.D. & J.L. Strimple, eds.) Cincinnati, OH.

1992 (with A. Leviton, S.C. Anderson & K.A. Adler) **Handbook to Middle East Amphibians and Reptiles.** Society for the Study of Amphibians and Reptiles, Oxford, OH, vi + 252 pp.

1992 **Serologic relationships among pit vipers: evidence from plasma albumins and immunodiffusion.** pp. 155–161. *In:* Biology of the Pit Vipers (J.A. Campbell and E.D. Brodine, Jr., eds.) Selva, Tyler, TX.

1992 **The life and times of sea snakes.** pp. 53–58 *In:* Collected Papers of the Tucson Herpetological Society (D.L. Hardy, ed.) Tucson, AZ.

1992 **The geckos of Malir.** The Monitor 4(2):1–3.

1992 **Malir II: some other lizards.** Ibid. 4(3):1–4.

1992 **Malir III: the snakes.** Ibid. 4(4):1–4.

1992 **Malir IV: cobras, frogs, and hedgehogs.** Ibid. 4(5).
1992 (with T.P. Simon, J.O. Whitaker & J.S. Castrale) **Checklist of the vertebrates of Indiana.** Proceedings of the Indiana Academy of Science 101:95–126.
1993 Preface to **The Venomous Sea Snakes** by W.A. Culotta & G.V. Pickwell. Krieger, Malabar, FL, 1993, pp. xi–xii.
1993 (Book review) **A Colour Atlas of Arthropods in Clinical Medicine by W. Peters, Wolfe, London, 1992.** New England Journal of Medicine 329:1511.
1994 **Belcher's sea snake and the deadliest snakes in the world.** Notes from NOAH (Northern Ohio Association of Herpetologists) 21(6):10–11.
1995 (with R.L. Norris) **Snake venom poisoning—what the herpetoculturist needs to know.** Vivarium 6 (6):4–9.
1995 (with R.L. Norris) **Non-North American venomous reptile bites.** pp. 710–730 *In:* Wilderness Medicine, 3rd ed., (P.S. Auerbach, ed.) Mosby Yearbook, St. Louis.
1995 (with H.B. Bechtel) **Arthropod envenomation and parasitism.** pp. 742–768 *In:* Wilderness Medicine, 3rd ed., (P.S. Auerbach, ed.) Mosby Yearbook, St. Louis.
1996 **Are there any nonvenomous snakes? An update on colubrid envenoming.** pp. 742–768 *In:* Advances in Herpetoculture (P.D. Strimple, ed.) International Herpetological Symposium, Des Moines, IA.
1996 **Bites by non-native venomous snakes in the United States.** Wilderness & Environmental Medicine 4:297–303.
1997 **History and status of herpetology in Indiana.** Proceedings of the Indiana Academy of Science 103:71–77.
1997 (with Dennis Brown) **Distribution and variation of the lizard *Cnemidophorus sexlimeatus* in Indiana.** Bulletin of the Chicago Herpetological Society 32:102–104.
1997 **Creepers, crawlers, and hoppers.** pp. 319–327 *In:*

The Publications of Sherman A. Minton, Jr.

The Natural Heritage of Indiana. (Marion T. Jackson, ed.) Indiana University Press, Bloomington.

1997 (with J. Malo Cisneros and B.M. de Cervantes) **Ophiophagy by an arthropod-eating snake.** Bulletin of the Chicago Herpetological Society 32:253.

1998 **Observations of Indiana amphibian populations: a forty-five year overview.** pp. 217–220 *In:* Status and Conservation of Midwestern Amphibians (M.J. Lannoo, ed.) University of Iowa Press.

1998 (with J. Malo Cisneros and B.M. de Cervantes) *Conopsis nasus:* **Reproduction.** Herpetological Review 29:170.

1999 **Geographic distribution.** *Pseudoeurycea scandens.* Herpetological Review 30 (1):49.

TAXA NAMED AFTER SHERMAN A. MINTON JR., AND MADGE R. MINTON

Coluber karelini mintonorum Mertens, 1969
Cyrtodactylus mintoni (Golubev and Szczerbak, 1981)
Proacris mintoni Holman 1961
***Typhlops madgemintonae* Khan, 1999a
***Typhlops madgemintonae shermani* Khan, 1999b

REFERENCES

Golubev, Michael L. and Nikolai N. Szczerbak. 1981. A new species of the genus *Gymnodactylus* (Reptilia, Gekkonidae) from Pakistan. Vestn. Zool. 1981(3):40–45 (in Russian).

Holman, J. Alan. 1961. A new Hylid genus from the Lower Miocene of Florida. Copeia 1961(3):354–355.

Khan, Muhammad Sharif. 1999a. *Typhlops ductuliformes* a new species of blind snakes from Pakistan and a note on *T. porrectus* Stoliczka, 1871 (Squamata: Serpentes: Scolecophidia). Pakistan Journal of Zoology 31(4):385–390.

Khan, Muhammad Sharif. 1999b. Two new species and a subspecies of blind snakes of genus *Typhlops* from Azad Kashmir and Punjab, Pakistan (Serpentes: Typhlopidae). Russian Journal of Herpetology 6(3):231–240.

Mertens, Robert. 1969. Die Amphibien und Reptilien West-Pakistans. Stuttgart. Beitr. Naturk. 197:1–96.

** See: Wallach, Van. 2000. Critical review of some recent descriptions of Pakistani *Typhlops* by M. S. Khan, 1999 (Serpentes: Typhlopidae). Hamadryad 25(2):129–143.